Paul Sams is a Partner at Dutton Gregory solicitors and practicing property Solicitor actively involved in residential and commercial development with a niche specialism in leasehold enfranchisement matters.

A Practical Guide to the Law of Enfranchisement and Lease Extension

2nd Edition

A Practical Guide to the Law of Enfranchisement and Lease Extension
2nd Edition

Paul David Sams
LLB Hons (silver badge in Cycling proficiency)
Solicitor
Specialist in all matters Conveyancing both
Residential and Commercial

Law Brief Publishing

Published 2022 by Law Brief Publishing, an imprint of Law Brief Publishing Ltd
30 The Parks
Minehead
Somerset
TA24 8BT

www.lawbriefpublishing.com

Paperback: 978-1-914608-36-0

Thank you to my wonderful wife Sarah for putting up with me. She is truly amazing and should be anointed a Saint.

Together we are a great team albeit one that does not always see eye to eye on everything. When we do not I freely admit I am usually (although not always) the one who is wrong.

PREFACE

Well if you are reading this book I am sorry this is not a crime thriller, a science fiction epic or a riveting biography of a great world leader. It is a book about the tantalising topic of lease extensions and enfranchisement. Having said that I can confirm that it is a page turner – I find it makes it easier to read if you turn the pages.

Who should read this book? Well everyone should really but I would say that wouldn't I? The book is aimed at the legal profession to give them some guidance on how to approach these areas of law. It is not intended to be a comprehensive in-depth study of each area as to be frank that would take up a huge volume of tomes on each topic. It is more of an instant guide to help those practicing in this area of law or connected to this area of law to know what they should be considering.

This is the second edition of this book so I do hope it is a sequel akin to 'The Empire Strikes Back' rather than 'Norbit 2'.

The law stated in this book is believed to be correct based on information available to me up to 30 December 2021.

Paul Sams
December 2021

CONTENTS

CHAPTER ONE

INTRODUCTION

To begin with one should keep in mind that this book only deals with leasehold property. If you own the freehold, it means that you own the building and the land it stands on outright, in perpetuity. It is your name in the land registry as "freeholder", owning the "title absolute", well most of the time but those exceptions to this rule are for another time. Some of the perceived advantages of owning a freehold as opposed to leasehold are:

- You won't have to pay annual ground rent
- You don't have a freeholder either failing to maintain the building, or charging large amounts for it
- The responsibility for maintaining the building rests with you as the freeholder

Houses tend to be freehold although as always there are some exceptions

So, what is leasehold? Leasehold means that you just have a lease from the freeholder (sometimes called the landlord) to use the home for many years. The leases are usually long term – often 90 years or 120 years and as high as 999 years – but can be short, such as 40 years.

- A lease gives the leasehold owner a contract with the freeholder, which sets down the legal rights and responsibilities of each party

- The freeholder will normally be responsible for maintaining the building, such as the communal areas, as well as the exterior walls and roof. However, other leaseholders might have claimed their "right to manage", in which case it is their responsibility. Conveniently this is dealt with later in this book.

- Leaseholders may more than likely have to pay maintenance fees, annual service charges and their share of the buildings insurance

- Leaseholders normally pay an annual "ground rent" to the freeholder

- Leaseholders will have to obtain permission for any majors works done to the property

- Leaseholders may face other restrictions, such as not owning pets or subletting

- If leaseholders don't fulfil the terms of the lease – for example, by not paying the fees – then the lease can become forfeit. This is a rare occurrence and many things prevent this happening in practice (mortgage lenders for a start tend to pay any arrears on items if there is a possibility that the lease could be forfeited to make sure that the security of their mortgage remains intact.

On this basis you may wonder why anyone would not buy freehold. Well practical reasons prevent the sale of everything as freehold. If you own a penthouse apartment at the top of a large block of flats, then if you own the freehold to just the same how would you have access to the same? Who would maintain the communal areas? How would it be insured? How would the owner of the shiny penthouse make sure that the other apartment owners did not do something that would affect the integrity or security of their property?

Leasehold solves this situation by allowing the owners in the block to have reciprocal rights/protections in place. The freehold acts more like a "wrapper" which contains all the leasehold properties within it.

As time goes by then a lease term decreases. As sure as night follows day, if you have something that is valid for a period of years then the same decreases in the amount of term remaining over time. As you would expect as the lease term gets shorter then this quite naturally influences the value of the lease itself. The shorter the lease the less likely it is to be attractive to buyers and mortgage lenders. Therefore, as the lease gets shorter the value gets lower.

The next chapter will consider the options regarding a lease extension that will become necessary at some point in the future if you don't want to be left with an asset that will revert to the freeholder at the end of the term. There is obviously a cost to the same and that can be affected by many factors which we will consider is some detail.

In addition, there are other considerations about leasehold property that I have touched upon above that we need to consider. If the terms of the lease are becoming short, then there remains the possibility that the leaseholders may wish to purchase the freehold. This will allow them to extend the lease on their terms at a lower cost. However, there will be a cost to purchasing the freehold. In addition, the freeholder may be doing something that the leaseholders disagree with or worse not doing anything at all, so they consider purchasing the freehold themselves then.

Another alternative is to form a Right to Manage Company to deal with the day to day management of the property without having to go to the cost of purchasing the freehold. Again, this is something we will consider later in this book.

We will have a look at a third way, an alternative to freehold and leasehold known as commonhold. This book will be another addition therefore to the pile of books regarding commonhold which will mean that there is one more book added to the list to outnumber the number of text books on commonhold compared to commonhold properties themselves.

The majority of the advice in this book relates to assisting lawyers in acting for the leaseholder or leaseholders in relation to the statutory (and non-statutory options) available to them. However, it seems only right to consider matters from the perspective of a freeholder including the options and rights that they have.

Well let's get started with looking at lease extensions, it will be enthralling…

CHAPTER TWO

VOLUNTARY LEASE EXTENSIONS

In this chapter we will look at voluntary as opposed to statutory lease extensions. The next chapter will, not surprisingly, be dedicated to statutory lease extensions. However before considering both we need to consider why a lease extension may be needed.

Residential leasehold property generally have terms between 99 to 999 years with lots of different terms in between. When I first started in the law I used to be thinner and I had more hair but also if a lease had at least fifty-five years remaining on the lease term when it was purchased that was considered "ok". This stemmed from the fact that most mortgage lenders would lend money on a 25-year term and they required 30 full years to be remaining on the term of the lease at the end of the mortgage.

To a large extent a lot of mortgage lenders still have that requirement in place. However quite a few require at least 70 years remaining at the time they lend. Some require more than that. From a practice point of view, I have seen the required term creep up over the years.

For some time now, I have been advising clients that if there are less than 90 years remaining then they should be concerned. Now this always does tend to surprise them given that is longer than most people live to. The issue stems from the magical term known as "marriage value".

Now this term does not relate to how much money a couple can make from being wed but the value attributed to a property once its lease has been extended. The key number of years remaining on the lease is 80 years. When the lease has less than 80 years remaining on the term than marriage value is considered, so the lease extension will cost considerably more.

Put simply, when you extend a lease that has less than 80 years to run, the marriage value comes into play. When a Lease is extended, it *adds value* to the property (well it should!), sometimes this can be a substantial amount. Under the 1993 Leasehold Reform Act, the landlord is entitled to *half* of the increase in the value of the property when a lease with less than 80 years remaining on the term is extended, this is called the Marriage value *or* Marriage fee, so-called because the value of the property plus a longer Lease (i.e. when Married together) exceed the combined value of the separate entities. When you extend a lease with a remaining term of 80 years *or more*, <u>no marriage fee is payable</u>.

You should always look to extend a lease before it hits the 80-year mark for this reason. If you don't warn your clients of the same when they purchase a property, then you face a negligence claim in relation to this. To this extent I have always adopted the approach of warning all clients purchasing leasehold property that they face these costs when the lease has less than 80 years remaining. Even if they are taking a new lease for say 125 years at the outset I think it is wise to always point out the above in your report letter.

To determine how much a lease extension will cost you then you can use one of the plethora of online calculators available, but if you want a definitive figure then you should speak to a surveyor who specialises in this area of law. The RICS have a list available of those who specialise in this area and I would strongly advise you to either forge a relationship with a couple of local experts or keep their contact details to hand to pass onto clients. Sadly, I have seen people end up agreeing to pay more than they needed to solely because they did not choose an expert.

Rather surprisingly a formal valuation is not actually required, so both freeholder and leaseholder can agree a figure between them. If it became contentious later though then having a formal valuation would be of benefit to have to hand if the matter must go to First Tier Property Tribunal. A good surveyor on your side will be able to negotiate with the freeholder's surveyor for you. It never ceases to amaze me how far apart parties can be with their valuations!

Now I have referred to the fact that when it comes time to extend a lease there are two options for a leaseholder – the voluntary option or statutory option. The statutory option comes from the Leasehold Reform Housing & Urban Development Act 1993 (as amended by subsequent Acts) which I have referred to briefly earlier. We will look at the Act in more depth in the next chapter.

Put simply, if voluntary terms can be agreed with the freeholder then the cost to your client and the work involved on your behalf should in theory be less than the statutory process. However, as the term implies it is completely voluntary and requires the freeholder to co-operate.

Some clients won't meet the criteria for a statutory extension, so the voluntary route remains their only chance to extend their lease. The first thing to remember is that there are no rules. The freeholder can offer you what they like. In addition, they may offer you an "amazing deal" but as always, the devil is in the detail.

For example, I have seen a large commercial freeholder offer lease extensions with no premium charged. Now on the face of this it sounds too good to be true. Sadly, this was the case. What the freeholder offered was no premium to be payable but ground rents to increase astronomically over the term of the lease. For example, they offered a new 125-year lease term with ground rent of £100.00 increasing every five years. Now this does not sound very much until you look at how the increases work. As follows:

1 – 5 years	£100
5 – 10 years	£200
10 – 15 years	£400
15 – 20 years	£800
20 – 25 years	£1,600
25 – 30 years	£3,200
30 – 35 years	£6,400
35 – 40 years	£12,800
40 – 45 years	£25,600
45 – 50 years	£51,200
50 – 55 years	£102,400
55 – 60 years	£204,800
60 – 65 years	£409,600
65 – 70 years	£819,200
70 – 75 years	£1,638,400
75 80 years	£3,276,800
80 – 85 years	£6,553,600
85 – 90 years	£13,107,200
95 – 95 years	£26,214,400
100 – 105 years	£52,428,800
105 – 110 years	£104,857,600
110 – 115 years	£209,715,200
115 – 120 years	£419,430,400
120 – 125 years	£838,860,800

When you see the figures laid out like this I am sure you will agree that the deal was not that much of a bargain. I have to admit though that secretly I do admire freeholders that have managed to do this. I know I should not but you have to admire that they had the where withal to spot these types of opportunities and take them. I know, I know, I will be going to the very hot sauna down below for admitting this but admiring the ability for an organisation to do this is not the same as condoning it.

A lot of lawyers will opt to persuade their clients to go down the voluntary route for selfish reasons – it is easier! The statutory route can lead to litigation and this is an area that is completely alien to most property lawyers. While that may have some validity, the fact that a voluntary lease extension is easier for the lawyer is not really a valid reason to choose this over another.

To be able to advise a client fully in the circumstances then, a lawyer must know the procedures and rules behind statutory lease extensions. Therefore, let us consider these in the next chapter.

CHAPTER THREE

STATUTORY LEASE EXTENSIONS

As mentioned previously, the piece of legislation that allows for this to happen is the Leasehold Reform Housing & Urban Development Act 1993 (as amended by subsequent Acts). Under the act then a leaseholder has an automatic right to require that their freeholder offer them an extension to their lease term. The extension itself is not for negotiation. By this I mean it is an addition of ninety years to the unexpired term with the ground rent reverting to a peppercorn rent.

Why a peppercorn I hear you say? Well historically, ground rent was typically very low, so as mentioned above freeholders would not find any value in collecting it. You might ask yourself, why did they not just set the ground rent to zero in the lease? Well, the reason for this is that for a lease contract to be considered legally binding, each side must provide 'consideration'. This means that both the freeholder and leaseholder must exchange something of value to the other party.

In the past, peppercorns were a valuable commodity like other spices, so it was deemed as absolute consideration to validate the lease contract. However, there are some leases in existence with even more unusual ground rents payable. These include one crab, a single red rose, one apple and a posy of flowers per annum. So, it would seem that freeholders became creative with their leases. As I have shown earlier freeholders can be very creative at times although more to maximise their "bottom line".

Who qualifies for this right?

If only it were that simple though. There are a couple of things to know to begin with. To be a qualifying leaseholder then the owner must have owned the property for more than two years. Without this two-year period of ownership then no statutory right exists, and the owner would be relying upon the freeholder's "good will" to consider granting a lease extension hence using the voluntary route.

In my experience it really does depend on the freeholder whether they are prepared to do this or not. Some will be reasonable and see the need for a lease extension as the lease is short so will agree terms as they know they will get a premium for the same. Sadly some, which again in my experience tend to be the larger commercial freeholders, take the view that they are in the business for the long term, so they will be looking to maximise the premium they can demand so why do it before the two-year qualifying period has been met?

It is possible to take a previous owner's qualifying period (assuming the previous owner had more than two years ownership at the time of sale). This can be achieved by having the seller serve the relevant notice on the freeholder following exchange but before completion then assigning the right to the new owner following this.

The other simple qualifying criterion (if we can call anything in the process simple) is that the lease is a long lease more than 21 years from when it was originally granted. The term of the lease at the point of extension is not relevant, it is the term at the time of creation. This is of course easy to verify.

However even if the leaseholder satisfies these criteria then they will not be a qualifying leaseholder if either of the following apply:

- the landlord is a charitable housing trust and the flat is provided as part of the charity's functions

- it is a business or commercial lease

In relation to the first point then again in my experience most such organisations will consider a lease extension on a voluntary basis. Their very reason for existence is to be beneficial to others so they will most likely consider offering the same.

Now the second point one would think is quite self evident. However, with the plethora of mixed use development sites in the past twenty years this may not be straightforward. For example, would a "live work unit" granted with the aim of having living accommodation above a business qualify? This could be an issue moving forward with time.

How do you start the process?

Assuming your client can meet the two criteria listed above then they need to start the process. How? Well let me enlighten you.

To commence with then your client will need to serve a section 42 notice under the 1993 Act aforementioned. This needs to be served on the party known as the competent landlord. A competent landlord is the landlord who is able to grant an extension to the lease term of ninety years. This means that they have to either serve on the freeholder or if there is a head lease serve the same upon the head leaseholder provided of course the head leaseholder has a lease that is longer than the lease that will be created.

For example, if the head leasehold only has one hundred years remaining on the term at the time of demanding the extension and the under lease only has fifty years remaining then this would be an issue. The new underlease would be for one hundred and forty years once extended which would be longer than the head lease. The head lease would expire before the underlease thus causing issues.

Now that you are aware of the above then the notice has to be prepared ready to be served. It needs to be served on all the landlords. By this I mean the freeholder and any other intermediate leases from which your clients underlease emanates. If there happens to be a management company created for the block that the flat is within then the notice should be served on them. They may have no more than a ceremonial function but many a time I have seen some commercial freeholders' solicitors reject a notice on the basis that the management company named in the lease was not named.

Now on to the notice itself.

Section 42 notice – first steps

One glaring item that needs to be within a section 42 notice is the tenant's offer for the premium of the lease extension. Now believe it or not the legislation does not specifically require a formal valuation to take place. However, should matters become contentious later then having a valuation from an expert surveyor as mentioned earlier is crucial. I would strongly urge you to make sure your clients follow this advice.

Once your client has provided you with a figure from their valuer then you need to set about gathering all the information that needs to be in the notice.

You will need to obtain the following information:

1. the identity of the competent landlord, a person, or company, name and address

2. details of any intervening or head leases and the identity and address of the relevant head lessees

3. a copy of clients own lease and the registered title

You should be able to identify the competent landlord from the ground rent demands, general correspondence you have received from them or if all else fails by checking the Land Registry (assuming the same is up-to-date). It never ceases to amaze me the number of freeholders that fail to register their title at the Land Registry. Some of the largest landlords are the worst at this.

Now you are asking what happens if the freeholder/landlord is absent? Well if that is the case I would refer you to the next chapter in this book which addresses the same.

Section 41 of the Act provides a right for leaseholders to serve notices on their immediate landlord, the freeholder (if different) or any other persons with an interest in the property, requiring details of that interest.

This information would include the name and address and of the freeholder or intermediate landlord and length of the lease and the extent of the premises.

The recipients of the Notices are required to respond within 28 days. The service of the Notices does not formally start the application for the new lease or commit you in any way and there is no liability for costs. If your client decides to back out at this stage, then it would have been wise to ensure you had monies on account of costs at the outset to at least cover your time/costs incurred.

The Notice triggers the statutory procedures for acquiring the new lease and the leaseholder is liable for the landlord's reasonable costs as from the date he received the Notice. It is therefore important that the Notice contains no inaccuracies or misdescriptions because, although these can be corrected by application to the County Court, it is an expense that should be avoided. An incomplete Notice can be rejected as invalid. Your client won't thank you if you get the same wrong and couple with this that it will of course set the wrong tone to the freeholders and their solicitors moving forward.

If the "competent landlord" is not the immediate landlord, then the original Notice will have to be served on the competent landlord and copies on the other landlords. The Notice to the competent landlord should specify to whom else a copy is being given. I have witnessed numerous times a notice being rejected because not all the relevant parties were served with a notice. The most common being the management company referred to within the lease itself.

A protection for leaseholders is the ability to register the Tenant's Notice with the Land Registry. This provides protection for the leaseholder against the landlord's sale of the freehold. Any purchaser of the freehold, after the registration of the Tenant's Notice will take the freehold subject to the application for the new lease. The procedure will therefore be able to continue as though the new owner had originally received the Tenant's Notice. You can register this using a Unilateral notice provided you have served the section 42 notice and make clear reference to this on the application form (i.e. sending a copy of the same with the application to the Land Registry.)

The service of the Tenant's Notice also fixes the "valuation date" as the same date as the Notice. The valuation date is when the variables affecting the price are set, for example, the remaining number of years left on the lease and the present value. Therefore, however long the negotiation or determination of the price takes it will be based on the factors applying on the date of service of the Tenant's Notice.

Again, this highlights the need to ensure that the notice is correct. If the notice must be reserved, then a further valuation will be needed for the later date. If for instance the lease had 80 years remaining on the term at the time the notice was served, then reserved after the same had slipped below 80 years then the cost of the premium would naturally rise for your client. Who do you think your client will look to for that increase in cost?

Serving the notice itself

The requirements of the Tenant's Notice are set out in S42(3) of the Leasehold Reform Housing and Urban Development Act 1993. It must contain the following:

- the full name of the leaseholder and the address of the flat – make sure this matches the details as per the Land Registry title for the property exactly;

- sufficient information about the flat to identify the property to which the application relates – I would suggest this should include the full Land Registry description of the property;

- details of the lease including its date of commencement and its terms – again exactly as per the Land Registry held lease or original lease if unregistered;

- the premium proposed for the new lease and or other amounts payable where there are intermediate leases involved – follow the advice of your client's chosen valuer – you are not qualified to give valuation advice no matter how tempted you feel to do so;

- the terms that the leaseholder proposes for the new lease; (if different from the present lease) – I would expect this to be the statutory offered terms as others will be queried unless favourable to the freeholder which would be highly unusual

- the name and address of his representative if one has been appointed – you should know your own contact details; and

- a date by which the landlord must give his Counter-Notice, which must be not less than two months from the date on which the Tenant's Notice is served – personally I always add five days to the time period just to make sure.

In relation to the premium quoted in the Notice, this may not be the price eventually agreed after negotiation or determined by the Tribunal (it would be highly bizarre if it was accepted), but it will be the figure from which the landlord calculates the deposit he requires. The premium proposed must be a realistic opening offer. Whilst it might be tempting to offer a satsuma and a packet of peanuts in order to reduce the amount of deposit required you should avoid this course of action. If you do offer a ridiculously low offer, then the Notice runs the risk of being found invalid. Again, who do you think your client would look to for any losses incurred for poor advice on serving an unrealistic valuation in the notice?

<u>So, the notice has been served – what next?</u>

After the service of the Tenant's Notice the landlord is entitled to require evidence of the leaseholder's title to the flat and his period of ownership. The landlord has a period of 21 days from the date of service of the Tenant's Notice in which to request the information.

Where this information is required it must be provided within 21 days. It is worth making a diary note of when 21 days is up from when you have served the notice to ensure you have a response. It also allows you to make sure you have not overlooked hearing from the freeholder or their solicitors. You should make sure you provide all the information regarding your clients' evidence of ownership. After all you will have the same on your file.

In the event that these are not met the landlord may serve a Default Notice and make application to the court for an order for compliance. Again, costs implications arise from this, so you need to make sure they are addressed.

The landlord also has the right to inspect the flat for the purposes of a valuation, subject to 3 days written notice to the tenant. You should ensure that your client is aware that a valuation may be required. If the property is rented to third party tenants under a rental agreement, then it may be an idea for your client to let the tenants know in advance (or their managing agents) as to why a valuation may be taking place.

It would be very unusual for a freeholder to not have a valuation carried out. They will look to your client to cover their surveyor's costs, so it is in their interest to have a valuation carried out to make sure that their interests are protected.

The landlord is entitled at any time after receipt of the Tenant's Notice to require the payment of a deposit. This may be 10% of the premium proposed in the Tenant's Notice or £250, whichever is the greater. Again, you should make your client aware of this before serving the notice and ensure you have the requisite sum in cleared funds from your client.

Prepare for the Landlord's counter notice

The landlord must serve his Counter-Notice by the date specified in the leaseholder's Notice; this must:

- agree the tenants right to the new lease and accept the terms offered (or propose alternative terms) – the latter is more likely, or

- not admit your right and give reasons, which will need to be determined by the county court – basically you got it wrong somehow, or

- claim right of redevelopment; the landlord can refuse to grant the new lease if he can prove to a court that he intends to demolish and redevelop the building. This only applies to applications where the remaining period of the lease is less than five years from the date when the notice was served. As you can imagine this is a very unusual reason for refusing to offer an extension.

Given that in most circumstances the leaseholder and the landlord cannot agree on the price or some other aspects of the conveyance, there is a statutory period for negotiation of at least two months but not more than six months. After the initial two months either party can apply to the Tribunal for an independent determination on the issue. We will look at the Tribunal application below.

In cases where the landlord fails to serve a Counter-Notice by the date specified in the Tenant's Notice (this does happen quite often) the leaseholder may apply to the court for a Vesting Order. This application is not for a court order requiring the landlord to serve the Counter-Notice but effectively takes the matter out of his hands in a request to the court to grant the new lease to the leaseholder in the landlord's default. The court will grant the Order on the terms proposed in the Tenant's Notice. The application must be made to the court within six months of the date on which the Counter-Notice should have been received. In some ways this is the best-case scenario from when a notice is served.

Once the Tenant's Notice has been served it may be assigned with the lease. This means that a leaseholder can serve the notice and then sell the flat with the benefits of the application. The purchaser will be able to proceed with the application immediately, without having to meet the two-year ownership qualification. This can be of assistance in cases where a present short term of lease presents mortgage difficulties for a prospective purchaser. You will need to ensure that the sale contract between the leaseholder and their buyer specifically refers to the fact that this is happening.

A tip I would advise all lawyers to follow if the benefit of the notice is going to be assigned is to ensure that whomever is acting for the buyer provides the assignment clause for the contract. This should provide that the buyer serves the notice on the freeholder between exchange and completion as Agent for the seller at this stage. To rely upon the seller's solicitors to do this, often someone who may not be confident in such matters opens you to a whole range of things to go wrong which your client will again look to you for.

In the sad event that a leaseholder who qualifies for the right to a new lease dies before making an application his personal representatives may exercise the right for a period of up to two years following grant of probate or letters of administration.

<u>Assuming it all goes well – what will my client receive?</u>

You should be aware of the legislative requirements for the terms on which the new lease is to be granted:

- to be at a peppercorn rent (i.e. no rent) for the whole of the term (the 90 years plus the present unexpired term)

- to be on the same terms as the existing lease, subject to minor modifications and certain statutory exclusions and additions:

- modifications – to take account of any alterations to the flat, or the building, since the grant of the existing lease (e.g. reference to gas lighting or coal stores), or to remedy a defect in the lease.

- exclusions – since the 1993 Act provides a right to perpetual renewal of the lease, any existing clauses relating to renewal, pre-emptions or early termination are to be excluded.

- additions – a requirement not to grant a sub-lease of sufficient length to confer on the sub-lessee a right to a new lease under the Act.

- the landlord's redevelopment right – the new lease must also contain a clause giving the landlord the right to repossession of the flat for the purposes of redevelopment. This right does not arise until the end of the term of the existing lease and is subject to a court application and the payment of full compensation to the leaseholder for the full value of the remaining 90 years. This will not cause any difficulties in mortgaging the flat.

It has not gone well, and we cannot agree a price – what next?

In some cases, a price cannot be agreed between the parties. This could be for a variety of reasons but usually it stems from the fact that the surveyors instructed by both parties cannot agree upon a figure that their respective clients find acceptable.

If this happens to your client, then the only option if they cannot negotiate is to make an application to First Tier Property Tribunal for the price to be determined by the Court. The process is relatively straightforward and requires a detailed application form (leasehold form 11). All the information required for the form you should have on file. The form also asks for a brief explanation of the terms that are in dispute.

It is possible to opt to ask the Tribunal to decide without a formal hearing. This will save your client the costs involved and having to attend a hearing, but it does require that all the other parties agree to the same. A commercial landlord is unlikely to agree to this as from a simple business perspective they want to achieve the highest premium possible for a lease extension so are likely to want "their day in court". They will have the finances to cover the cost of the same and it acts as an indicator to other leaseholders that they will act robustly when it comes to extending their leases too.

The form itself (as most Court forms do) comes with a useful checklist attached which sets out the following requirements:

- That the form has been completed in full – if not it will automatically be rejected

- A copy of the required documents – this will be a copy of everything you have on your file including a copy of the notice and your client's valuation

- Additional copies of the form to send to the other parties

- A cheque for £100.00 being the court fee

If a hearing is requested/required, then a further £200.00 fee will be due.

Appearing at Tribunal is probably the last thing that your client wishes to incur the costs of, but it would be wise to make them aware at the very outset of the costs involved. If you are not prepared to appear on behalf of your client, then if you seek either a colleague or Counsel to deal with the same then their costs will need to be factored in.

Next steps

Once the price has been agreed, either by negotiation or by a Tribunal then the lease itself must be agreed. This should be relatively straightforward. However please take care when the same is received from the freeholder's solicitors to make sure there are no "hidden extras" within the same.

Procedures and Statutory time limits summing up

- leaseholder serves S41 Information Notice (discretionary)
- Landlord must respond within 28 days
- leaseholder serves S42 Tenant's Notice
- The "valuation date" will be fixed as the date of service of the S42 Tenant's Notice
- Landlord may request additional information, but they must do so within 21 days of receipt of the Tenant's Notice
- leaseholder's must respond to his request within 21 days
- Landlord must serve a Counter-Notice by the date specified in the notice. This date must be at least two months from the date of service of the Tenant's Notice
- Where the landlord fails to serve the Counter-Notice

leaseholders must apply to court within six months for a vesting order

- After service of the Counter-Notice either party may apply to the Tribunal). This must be done no sooner than two months from, but within six months of, the date of service of the Counter-notice

- The application fee to the Tribunal is £100 and the hearing fee (on receiving notice of a hearing date) is £200.

- The Tribunal determination becomes final after 28 days. Appeals must be made within this period to the Lands Tribunal but only with the leave of the Tribunal

- After the Tribunal decision is final landlord must provide draft lease within 14 days

- Period of two months after decision becomes final for parties to enter into the new lease

- If the period above elapses without entry into new lease, then leaseholder must apply to court within a further two months requiring the Landlord to meet his obligations

The statutory process may seem daunting at first. To most property lawyers it will be as it involves "paperwork" that is more akin to litigation, but I hope that I have set out here that it is nothing actually to be afraid of. The key to any successful legal matter is to make sure that things are done promptly, on time and in the right order. If the procedure set out within the Act is followed, then you should not have any issue.

Absent freeholders

A lot of leaseholders I have met over the years seem actually to be quite happy that they don't know who their freeholder is or where they are. Often, I have been quoted "it's great as I don't get charged for service charge or the ground rent". Well the immediate gratification of not having to find monies to cover the upkeep of the building or being smug in quoting that only six years' worth of unpaid ground rent can be claimed is all well and good, until that happy leaseholder comes to sell. The fact that they have say less than seventy years on the lease when they come to sell so they cannot secure a buyer tends to remove the glee at not having paid the mundane service charges etc.

Now in the modern technologically advanced world in which we live, where it seems we can order any item we want and have it delivered to a destination of our pleasure then tracking someone down should be easy. The likes of social media should make this a straightforward task.

Sometimes it is not possible to find someone no matter how hard you look. However before commencing any process to try and extend a short lease then steps have to be taken to try and find the absent freeholder. Evidence of the same is going to need to be seen of these steps.

If the freeholder cannot be traced, then rather than having to tell your now distraught leaseholder that they cannot extend their lease you can safely tell them that they have options. I should mention at this stage that it is possible to purchase legal indemnity insurance at a relatively low cost to cover issues associated with an absent freeholder. However contrary to what I have had to explain to clients on more than one occasion this does not extend cover to granting a new lease!

Quite often I have discovered that the freeholder has been absent as the management company/freehold company set up to own the freehold has become defunct. It has either been struck off at Companies House for failure of statutory requirements being (no accounts being filed etc) or the company has fallen into receivership.

If the company that owns the freehold has ceased to exist then it is possible to resurrect the same via the Treasury solicitors and carry out a lease extension that way. This would only apply where a company that owned the freehold that the leaseholder had an interest within.

Again, then if a company that owns the freeholder has fallen into receivership then the leaseholder can serve a notice against the receiver. The same would apply if the freeholder was owned by an individual who had been made bankrupt, a notice could be served against their Trustee in Bankruptcy.

Any Receiver or Trustee in Bankruptcy would be stepping into the shoes of the freeholder so would be bound by the 1993 Act to respond and act in the same way as if the original party was. The notices would just need to be served against them, not the named freeholder. The process (save for the name of the parties) would be as described in the previous chapters.

Now if the freeholder cannot be found at all then you may think all is lost. Well it is not. In these circumstances an application to the County Court can be made. This was set out within the 1993 Act as those responsible for drafting the Act clearly had some foresight into this type of problem arising.

To obtain a vesting order a leaseholder seeking to extend their lease or a group of leaseholders wanting to buy the freehold or claim their right to manage (see later chapters on this topic) merely need to make an application to the County Court. Such an application should be made on a CPR Part 8 application form and the Court fee is around £150.00.

If the County Court is to grant a vesting order they must be satisfied that reasonable efforts to trace the landlord have been made.

Evidence of such efforts could include:

- a land registry search of the Freeholder's last known address to prove that they no longer own the property and have moved on to address unknown,

- witness statements to confirm that a visit to the Freeholder's last known address has not provided a forwarding address, or

- an absentee freeholder title indemnity policy that may have been taken as a condition of mortgage by any leaseholder who recently bought a flat in the block. Although I may have sounded mocking against such policies earlier in this chapter they do have a significant use.

The particulars of claim will need to set out whether the hopeful leaseholder or leaseholders have served their notice of claim on the Freeholder's last known address or served such notice in the London Gazette or a local paper or a request that the Court grants a dispensation from the requirement to serve notice. It never ceases to amaze me that notices are so required in the London Gazette when very few people will now read the same. Ask yourself, when was the last time you read the same?

The Court will need to include up to date Land Registry title searches, copy leases, copy notices, witness statements, draft land registry transfer forms and other matters highlighted above.

The County Court may set a date for a hearing or the district judge may be satisfied that reasonable efforts to trace the Freeholder have been made and rule on the basis of the facts as presented to them, without need for a hearing. If the Judge is satisfied with the evidence provided, the Court will issue a judgment setting out that the freehold may be acquired by the leaseholder(s) with funds to be 'vested' in the Court and deferring the case to the First-tier Tribunal (Property Chamber) (formerly the Leasehold Valuation Tribunal ('LVT')) for determination of a 'reasonable' premium.

The First-tier Tribunal (Property Chamber) also hears many absentee Freeholder cases without a full hearing by issuing directions for the hopeful leaseholders to comply with and timescales for documents to be produced by. The documents the Tribunal will need include the order made by the County Court, copy leases, the valuation for the leaseholders, and proposed land registry transfer form.

The Tribunal panel usually consists of a layperson, a solicitor experienced in such matters and a valuer who make their determination from not only the evidence put before them but also their experience. Therefore, it is imperative that a formal valuation be prepared and presented. The Tribunal will not accept unsubstantiated figures at this stage.

Now when explaining the above to a leaseholder I imagine that one of the first things they would ask is whether this is going to be expensive. I don't propose to suggest what you charge your clients, but the process is not as complicated or as oppressive as it may sound.

It is worth pointing out that you may save the cost of serving a Section 42 Claim Notice and you will save the cost of negotiations with the Freeholder's Surveyor because there is no-one to negotiate with as the First-tier Tribunal will determine the case. There will be no freeholder's solicitor's fees or freeholder's surveyor's fees to pay either.

The disadvantage is that although there is no one to negotiate with then there is always the chance that a lower figure could have been agreed upon.

There are many out there who have been told by their local expert, Dave down the Dog and Duck Public House, that this is an easy process. I hope I have shown now that it is not akin to climbing Everest but still requires a fair amount of work which a leaseholder needs to be prepared to pay for. The future though could change all of this.

In July 2020 the Law Commission published three reports in relation to Property within England and Wales. They related to leasehold property, Right to Manage companies and Commonhold. I will look at the latter two issues in later chapters but for now let us take a look at what was proposed in relation to lease extensions.

The main suggestions that the Law Commission have suggested can be summed up here:

- Giving leaseholders the chance to "buy out" their ground rent provisions without having to go to the expense of extending their lease

- That when a leasehold property is sold then if an application has been made to extend the lease that the same should pass automatically to the buyer (unless they do not want to take that on) rather than having the rigmarole of making sure that the benefit is assigned correctly

- That a leaseholder should not have to pay the landlord's costs involved with an application

It is worth keeping in mind that all of these are just suggestions. However the Government have brought forward a Leasehold Reform (Ground Rent) Bill in 2021, at the time of writing this has not yet passed. What this proposes is that all new property should have a peppercorn ground rent and lease extensions will be for nine hundred and ninety years as opposed to ninety years. It is worth noting that the main national developers have all adopted peppercorn ground rents and nine-hundred and ninety-nine year leases for new properties in the past few years.

Well having looked at lease extensions in some depth there is another alternative to explore for your clients if they come to you with a short lease. This is to see if purchasing the freehold is a viable option which we will now look at within the next chapter.

CHAPTER FOUR

ENFRANCHISEMENT

So, you have spent some time explaining to your client about their options regarding lease extensions. Now logic dictates that if their lease needs extending then others within the block where the property is located will need to be extended at the same time because all the leases should be on identical terms.

An alternative to obtaining a lease extension is to consider whether your client leaseholder and their fellow leaseholders would like to exercise their right under the 1993 Act to purchase the freehold to their building themselves. In the long run the likelihood is that owning the freehold to the block where the leasehold property is located will save the leaseholder money as in theory they will have control over what happens with their building more than if another owns the freehold. The larger managing agents and freeholders make monies from all the tasks they have to carry out at premises, not just their fee which usually equates to a large percentage of any service charge. For example, they will be able to negotiate a more favourable rebate on insurance and works that are required when dealing with multiple freeholds compared to a single building.

The biggest issue I find when speaking to clients about enfranchisement is that like most ideas that involve a group of people, there will be those who lead a process at the beginning that others say they will join. After time and reflection that enthusiasm to join in begins to wane. When say everyone agreed to go ahead within a block to purchase the freehold to a building then when the issue of money arises I have always found that some of those involved begin to change their mind.

The secondary issue that arises when you need to have multiple people agreeing to a course of action is that some decide to take the lead then when monies become involved everyone wants a say. For instance, imagine if you have fifty participants in a freehold purchase and they all insist on meeting with you. They all want to call you, they all want their emails responded to and they all want you to treat them as an individual. This is all before they all start giving conflicting instructions. Sound like fun? Have you ever tried to herd cats? When I go out for dinner with my wife (rarely I admit) it can take her quite a while to choose what to eat. That is one couple trying to agree on something. Imagine what it will be likely with multiple parties who will all be completely different save they happen to live in the same block of flats.

Participation agreement

Forgive me for my sentiments in my previous section as quite often everyone within a block is united in their aim to own the freehold so a harmonious group with clear instructions will be before you. However, I would always suggest to any group before me that they should consider setting out an agreement between the parties wishing to participate.

This is more commonly referred to as a "Participation Agreement". It sets out who will be involved, everyone's obligations to each other, will usually name one or two people who will lead the negotiations and perhaps most importantly what financial contributions all will have to make. The agreement can also make provision for non-participating leaseholders to join in at a later stage.

I would suggest that any agreement ensures that the following are always covered:

- Who is participating?
- Who is going to take the lead in the process? (this will make your life easier of course)
- That regular payments will be made (this is vital)
- That all will contribute towards the purchase price of the freehold when the time comes
- That none of the participants will do anything to invalidate the claim
- That if any of the participants should withdraw then they accept responsibility for their share of the costs

To quote the Act, Section 28 (4) of the Leasehold Reform, provides that the participating tenants are liable to the landlord for all costs incurred from the Initial Notice until when the claim is withdrawn. Liability for costs is "joint and several". This means the landlord can recover its costs from any participating tenant, so the importance of the Participation Agreement is to protect everyone involved. This will stop one individual leaseholder from being presented with a claim from the landlord for all the costs in the case if there was no Participation Agreement and other leaseholders refuse to pay.

Having the Participation Agreement in place will save disputes at a later date and will ensure that you have funds ready to proceed with matters. Please keep in mind though that there is no automatic right for all of the owners of leasehold properties within the block to participate. It is purely voluntary if they wish to take part or not. I certainly think this is worth mentioning to whomever is leading the process. Too often I have seen scenarios where one or two owners think that if they lead the way then other leaseholders have to automatically follow. This is not actually the case.

Agreement signed? Monies on account? Everyone contributed that you need to for your costs? Let's look at what to do next in the process.

Opening negotiations

As with lease extensions the statutory route is not the only one to consider taking. It is possible that if your clients have a willing freeholder who wishes to sell then the process will be slightly more straightforward. You should probably still consider advising your clients to have a Participation Agreement to make sure that everyone is clear on how matters will proceed. It is always worth speaking to the freeholder first to see if they are open to selling as once a notice is served under the statutory process then costs are incurred. Sometimes the freeholder wishes to sell (see later in this chapter regarding section five notices)

If your clients have a commercial landlord, then it is unlikely that they will wish to sell the freehold. The freehold is likely to be one of many that they own, and they derive income from the same. Would you sell if you were them?

Every lease within a block is of value to the freeholder because:

- They are most likely receiving income from the ground rent from the property – it is no coincidence that many major pension funds purchase freeholds as they are considered a safe stable long-term investment

- That when the lease becomes shorter then a lease extension will be required which will result in a premium being paid to the freeholder

- Holds a reversionary interest – in theory the lease will one day expire so the apartment will revert back to the freeholder

- There may be development potential from the land surrounding the block, from the roof space, the car park area etc

- They will be making commission from carrying out the management tasks as I have alluded to above

Therefore, your clients will need a formal valuation from an expert to ascertain the value. Oddly enough the Act itself does not require a formal valuation but it would be foolish to enter into any form of negotiation (statutory or otherwise) without being armed with a valuation from a surveyor to add credence to any offer your clients make. Again Dave from the Dog and Duck giving you his expert opinion as a panel beater on valuations will not look great before the First Tier Property Tribunal if it goes that far.

Without wishing to stray into the area of specialism of a valuer it is important that you grasp the following issues that affect the valuation elements of a freehold:

- The number of leasehold properties within the freehold

- The market value of each apartment considering the term remaining on each of the leases

- The value of the freeholder's interest by calculating the ground rent received and the reversionary value of each leasehold property at the end of their respective lease terms

- The marriage value as discussed earlier

- The value from other income as discussed above

- Any "Appurtenant Property". This is defined in Section 1 (7) of the 1993 Act as:

"*appurtenant property*", in relation to a flat, means any garage, outhouse, garden, yard or appurtenances belonging to, or usually enjoyed with the flat."

So, you know your clients need a formal valuation, that you should have a Participation Agreement in place and your clients have tried to negotiate on a "friendly" basis with their freeholder but the freeholder won't respond. At this stage you will need to consider using the statutory route to approach the freeholder. Before doing so it is worth considering what the criteria under the Act are.

Criteria under the Act

This should be obvious, but you need to confirm that the building qualifies. The building must contain:

- At least two residential flats

- At least two thirds of the residential flats are owned by "Qualifying Tenants"

A Qualifying Tenant is an owner of a leasehold apartment where there was more than twenty-one years on the term of the lease when first granted. The same requirement as for a statutory lease extension so no surprise there.

There are other leases that come within the definition of a qualifying tenant, these are rare though being:

- a shorter lease which contains a clause providing a right of perpetual renewal;

- a lease terminable on death or marriage or an unknown date (including the so-called 'Prince of Wales' clauses – these are where the term comes to the end at irregular intervals linked to deaths or weddings within the British monarchy);

- the continuation of a long lease under the Local Government Housing Act 1989 following the expiry of the original term;

- a shared ownership lease where the tenant's share is 100% (this is not really that rare but see below as to the issue with shared ownership);

- A lease granted under the 'right to buy' or 'right to acquire on rent to mortgage terms'.

However as always there are exceptions to these. Even if the leaseholder satisfies the above criteria, they will not be a qualifying tenant if any of the following cases apply:

- the landlord is a charitable housing trust and the flat is provided as part of the charity's functions;

- the tenant owns more than two flats in the building. This is either jointly with others or solely in their own name. Please note where this applies these flats will be discounted from the two-thirds (we will look at ownership rules again later in this chapter);

- the tenant has a business or commercial lease (this should be obvious to work out but again I would refer to "Live Work Units".)

If more than 25% of the internal floor area of the building, excluding any common parts, is neither used or intended to be used for residential purposes then the building will not qualify. This could be shops, offices etc. Please note garages and parking spaces specifically used by flats in the building will be classed as residential.

There is no right of collective enfranchisement where: -

- the building is a conversion into four or fewer flats and
- not a purpose-built block; and
- the same person has owned the freehold since before the conversion of the building into flats; and
- he or an adult member of his family has lived there for the past 12 months.

Some properties are completely excluded from the rights of lease extension and collective enfranchisement:

- buildings within a cathedral precinct;
- National Trust properties;
- The freehold includes any track of an operational railway, including a bridge or tunnel or retaining wall to a railway track;
- Crown properties. Although the Crown is not bound by the legislation, the Government has made a statement to the House of Commons that the Crown will be prepared to comply with the principles of it.

So, you have established that the building qualifies, and you have qualifying tenants. A further hurdle exists. You need to check that you have enough qualifying leaseholders prepared to participate in the acquisition of the freehold.

The minimum number of participating tenants must equal half the total number of flats in the building; for example, if there are 10 flats in the building, at least five of the flats of qualifying tenants must participate in the action. If there are only two flats within the block, then both must participate.

Who is going to be the purchaser?

Well now you have established that your clients meet the criteria, that you have enough leaseholders agreeing to join in and you have a signed Participation Agreement with monies on account. You need to choose a nominated purchaser for the notice which will be served on the freeholder.

The Nominee purchaser can be anyone. It can be one of the tenants, a corporate person or a Trust. Usually it will make more sense for those taking part to form a limited company then each own a stake (by share or guarantee). There are currently no controls or qualifications in the legislation governing selection of Nominee Purchasers and the tenants are free to choose whoever or whatever agency they wish.

So now we know who is going to purchase what should you do next. Serving the notice on the freeholder. Shall we now look at that?

Serving the notice on the freeholder

The information required to be able to allow you to serve the notice on your client's behalf is not at all dissimilar to that needed to be able to be able to prepare a notice that your client wishes to extend their lease under statutory terms.

You will need to obtain the following information:

- the identity of the freeholder(s) – a person or company name and address;
- details of any intervening or headleases and the identity and address of the relevant lessees;
- the full names and addresses of all the leaseholders of the building and details of their leases;
- details of any flats in the control of the landlord and let on periodic tenancies.

Most of this information you should have on your file or can be obtained from a little bit of research mainly from the Land Registry.

Under the Act Leaseholders are entitled to obtain details of the name and address of their landlord under rights provided by the Landlord and Tenant Act 1985. The information, if requested must be provided within 21 days and failure to do so is an offence. Any ground rent demands should also carry the same details. It may be though that there are intermediate leases between the tenants' leases and the freeholder. These leases may not actually have any contact with the leaseholders.

If this is the case then section 11 of the Act provides a right for tenants to serve notices on the freeholder, the landlord (if different) or any other persons with an interest in the property, requiring details of that interest.

You can therefore require from the landlord details of any other freeholders, any intermediate leases, including the name and address of the lessee and the terms of the lease. The Information Notices can also require sight of relevant documents, for example, giving details of service charges or surveys. Those that receive the

Notices are required to respond within 28 days. The service of the Information Notice does not formally start the enfranchisement process or commit the tenants in any way and there is no liability for costs.

Once you have established to whom you will be sending the notice (of if there are intermediate leases – notices) then it is time to prepare the same.

What should the notice contain?

The initial notice is the starting pistol on the procedure, so it needs to be correct. False starts will mean returning to the start again which will incur you the wrath of your clients and may affect your ability to claim your fee. It is possible to correct errors by applying to the County Court, but one imagines your clients won't be happy to cover the cost or time involved with the same.

You need to ensure that at this stage your clients are certain they wish to proceed. Once the notice is served then reasonable costs can be demanded from the freeholder, after all they are doing something they don't have to or necessarily want to do.

So now you have the go ahead to proceed from your clients you need to serve the notice as prescribed under section 13 of the Act.

It is important to remember that the date of the notice is important for two reasons. Firstly, a strict timetable begins on the date of service, and secondly, it sets the valuation date for determining the price.

The notice must:

- Specify or provide a plan showing the premises (and any other appurtenant property or common parts, and any of the freeholder's property over which it is proposed rights should be granted) of which the freehold is proposed to be acquired;

- State the grounds on which it is claimed that the specified premises are, on the relevant dates, premises to which the right to enfranchise applies;

- Specify any leasehold interests which are proposed to be acquired;

- Specify any flats or other units subject to a mandatory leaseback;

- Specify the proposed purchase price of i. The freehold of the specified premises and ii. The freehold of the appurtenant property

- Give details of all the qualifying tenants in the premises;

- State the details, including address for service, of the purchaser;

- Specify the date by which the reversioner must respond (this date should be at least two months from the date upon which the notice is given);

- If copies are being given to any other relevant landlord and if so to name them. Until recently (May 2014), the initial notice had to be signed personally by each of the tenants. This is no longer the case and most notices will be signed by the acting solicitor so check that you have!

So now you have served the notice then it should be protected against the freeholder and any intermediate title holders legal title at the Land Registry.

Protecting the notice

Registering the notice is vitally important. This is for two reasons: first the registration of the initial notice has consequences under section 19 of the Act; and second, to protect the priority of the enfranchisement claim under the Land Registration Act 2002. This should be done as soon as to the initial notice is served.

Section 97(1) of the Act provides that a notice under section 13 shall be registrable under the Land Charges Act 1972 (in the case of unregistered land) or may by the subject of a notice under the Land Registration Act 2002 as if it were an estate contract. Section 19(1) prevents the severing of the landlord's interest or the grant of any further lease after the relevant date. This therefore "freezes" the interests in the property so that the scheme of the 1993 Act can have proper effect.

Section 19 (2)-(3) ensures that on any disposal of the freehold or other relevant interest the new owner or assignee will be bound by the initial notice and any other steps that have been taken in the collective enfranchisement process. This protects the tenant's claim against any subsequent dispositions of the landlord's property. The later effect is also supported by the Land Registration Act 2002. Where there is a notice on the registered title, that notice ensures that the priority of the enfranchisement claim is protected even if there is a registered disposition of the registered estate made for valuable consideration: section 29(1) and (2)(a)(i) of the Land Registration Act 2002. The right of a tenant arising out of the initial notice is not an overriding interest under paragraphs 2 of Schedules 1 and 3 of the Land Registration Act 2002. However, the effect of section 97(1) of the Act is to enable a notice to be entered in relation to the initial notice as if it were an estate contract. If the initial notice is not registered and there is a disposition of the landlord's interest, the new owner will not be bound by the initial notice

It is worth considering the fascinating case of Curzon v Wolstenholme [2015] UKUT 0173 (Lands Chamber) an initial notice was not protected by registration. The owner of the freehold sold his interest to his wife for £1.00 after the initial notice had been served by the tenants. Mr Curzon then had the freehold transferred back to him again from his wife for no consideration whatsoever. The Court described Mr Curzon as providing "determined opposition".

Brief facts of the case are that sufficient numbers of leaseholders wished to purchase the freehold. The surveyors for both parties agreed broad terms for the price in 2007. There were a few minor points to be agreed but the surveyors agreed that on these points then both parties would abide by whatever decision the Tribunal would make. Mr Curzon then successfully stalled for time until October 2012 when he transferred the freehold to his wife. She transferred it back in March 2013.

The section 13 notice was not protected at the Land Registry by way of notice. If it had been it would have alerted the leaseholders to the freehold transfer. There is no denying that Mr Curzon was trying to invalidate the notice that he had received.

It was accepted by all parties that the initial notice did not bind the wife because of the want of registration. However, the wife then transferred the freehold back to her husband by way of a gift. The Upper Tribunal had to determine whether the first transfer resulted in the initial notice having no effect whatsoever, or whether it could still bind the original freehold owner (the husband). The Upper Tribunal (Lands Chamber), held that while it was correct that the absence of registration meant that the initial notice did not bind the wife, it did still affect the original freeholder.

However, the Court of Appeal held that the lower Courts had

wrongly interpreted the law in holding that the initial notice remained enforceable against Mr Curzon following the re-transfer of the reversion. Firstly, it was pointed out that it was uncontroversial that a notice was not enforceable against the transferee of the reversion and that it was therefore not necessary to make an application to withdraw the notice against the transferor in order to serve a fresh notice against the transferee.

The Court of Appeal rejected the argument that s.9 of the Act referred to the reversioner at the time when the initial notice was served. Therefore, the words "in connection with any claim to exercise the right to collective enfranchisement" in s.9 could not be interpreted so as to resurrect the initial notice upon re-transfer. The notice had to be correct first time and protected at that time.

It was further held that the lower Courts wrongly interpreted the law in holding that s.13(11) was exhaustive in its enumeration of the circumstances in which a notice ceases to have effect. By way of example, a notice will cease to have validity when the proceedings to which it relates are struck out. The Court was of the view that even if s.13(11) were exhaustive, the notice would not be enforceable against Mr Curzon due to a combination of s.19(2), (3) and s.97(1) because the tenants' rights were not protected with the Land Registry.

The thing to take from this case is that notices once served need to be protected by way of notice at the Land Registry against the freeholder's title(s). If this is not carried out, then the acting solicitors face a claim of professional negligence as they won't have acted in their clients' best interests.

So once the notice is served and protected. What happens next? Before that though, what happens if you cannot find anyone to serve the notice on?

Absent freeholder/landlord

The whole process is not dissimilar at all to the process to be followed for a statutory lease extension with an absent freeholder. If the freeholder cannot be found, this should not prove an obstacle to enfranchisement; the issue can be resolved by either:

- if the freeholder was a company which has been struck off, or ceased to trade for some other reason, its property may have passed to the Crown through the Treasury Solicitor. Enquiries should be made of the Treasury Solicitor who will usually be prepared to sell the freehold to the tenants at open market value. This must be done by negotiation and there is no need (or legal ability) to serve the Initial Notice. This is a relatively easy process.

- if the freeholder is a company in receivership, then the Initial Notice may be served on the Receiver; similarly, if the owner is an individual who is bankrupt, the Notice may be served on the Trustee in Bankruptcy. Both the Receiver and the Trustee are acting as landlord for the time being and are equally bound by the Act to respond, as landlord, in the service of a Counter-Notice and sale of the freehold.

- if the freeholder just cannot be found then the Initial Notice cannot be served. In this case, the tenants may make application to the county court for a Vesting Order. They must make reasonable efforts to find the freeholder first. This can include placing an advertisement in a local and national newspaper amongst other options.

If the court is satisfied with the efforts made and qualification, then it will, in effect, sell the freehold to the tenants in the freeholder's absence. This is subject to application to the First-tier Tribunal (Property Chamber) ("the Tribunal") for determination of the price. The price is paid to the County Court. The benefit being that with an absent freeholder there is no need to prepare for negotiation on price or to prepare for a counter notice.

Assuming you have a freeholder then the freeholder is likely to reply to your notice to either agree or disagree with the notice. So, the "game begins".

Counternotice

Once the freeholder has your notice they have twenty-one days to request evidence of the participating leaseholders' legal titles to their properties to ensure that they are entitled to participate.

The leaseholders (or more importantly you as their legal advisor) have twenty-one days from receiving the notice to comply with the request for information. I would suggest that you make a diary reminder to ensure that you do this and to be aware that the request is likely to be forthcoming. If the information is not supplied within the time frame or part of the information is not supplied and by failing to do so, then that person participating would have been required for the notice (too few joining in for instance) then the notice is considered withdrawn.

If the notice is withdrawn, then the leaseholders serving the notice are liable to pay any costs due to the freeholder. In addition to that "punishment" a new initial notice cannot be served for twelve months from the date of the original withdrawal. Again, if you don't get this right then the tenants will not be happy and will likely look to you for any wasted costs and much worse, most likely the increase in price of purchasing the freehold in the future.

Given that you will have ensured that the notice is correct then the freeholder must respond by the date you have provided within the initial notice. The counternotice must contain the following:

- agree your right to the freehold and accept the terms you have offered (or propose alternative terms); or

- claim to reject your right and give reasons why not (which will then need to be determined by the county court); or

- *neither* admit nor deny entitlement, but state that an application is to be made to court for an order that the right to enfranchise cannot be exercised on the grounds the freeholder intends to redevelop the whole or a substantial part of the premises (we will consider this further below);

- any leaseback proposals must be specified (again we will look at this in more depth below)

Redevelopment ground for stalling enfranchisement

The freeholder will not be obligated to sell the freehold if they can prove to the court that they intend to demolish and redevelop the whole or a substantial part of the building. This can only apply where at least two-thirds of all the leases in the building are due to terminate within a period of five years from the date of service of the Initial Notice. It is unlikely that any freeholds you will be dealing with will be this short in relation to the lease term. However, it is worth knowing nevertheless in the case of a freeholder using this "excuse" to avoid enfranchisement on perhaps an unsuspecting lawyer not being aware of the terms of the Act.

Leaseback ground for stalling enfranchisement

Where the freeholder owns a flat, or flats, in the building which are not let to a qualifying tenant, he has the option of taking a leaseback on the flat(s) on a 999-year lease. A local authority freeholder or

Housing Association must take a leaseback where they have a "secure tenant "in one or more flats in their building.

Where there is a leaseback the value of the flat(s) is deducted from the calculations. Where, after service of the freeholder's Counter-Notice, the proposed purchaser and the freeholder cannot agree on the price or some other points of the final transaction, then after the initial two months, following service of the Counter-Notice, either party can apply to the Tribunal for an independent determination on the issue. If this occurs, then you will need to ensure that you have everything ready to go to Tribunal including ensuring that the surveyor involved is prepared to be questioned on their valuation.

What happens when the freeholder fails to serve a counter notice correctly?

In cases where the freeholder fails to serve a Counter-Notice by the date specified in the Initial Notice, the participating leaseholders may apply to the county court for a Vesting Order. This is an order allowing them to acquire the freehold on the terms of the Initial Notice (including the premium proposed). The court, if satisfied of the right to enfranchise, will grant the Order. The application must be made to the court within six months of the date on which the Counter-Notice should have been received. This is very similar to the process we looked at earlier regarding statutory lease extensions.

Procedures and Statutory time limits summing up

- Leaseholders serve section 11 Information Notice (discretionary).
- Freeholder must respond within 28 days to the section 11

Information Notice.

- Leaseholders must make arrangements for a Nominee Purchaser (enter into a Participation Agreement) and, if forming a company, register the same at Companies House.

- The initial section 13 notice is served.

- The 'valuation date' will be fixed as the date of service of the S13 Initial Notice.

- The Freeholder may request evidence of the title of participating leaseholders, but he must do so within 21 days of receipt of the Initial Notice.

- The Purchaser must respond to his request within twenty-one days. If he does not respond, then the notice is deemed invalid and cannot be served for at least another twelve months from the date of rejection.

- The Freeholder must serve a Counter-Notice by the date specified in the Notice. This date must be at least two months from the date of service of the Initial Notice. Where the freeholder fails to serve the Counter-Notice, the Purchaser must apply to court within six months for a Vesting Order, otherwise the Initial Notice is deemed withdrawn.

- If the Counter-Notice disputes qualification, the Purchaser must apply to the court, within two months of Counter-Notice, for declaration that Initial Notice is valid. After service of the Counter-Notice, if terms cannot be agreed, either party may apply to the Tribunal. This must be done at least two months from, but within six months of, the date of service of the Counter-Notice.

- The application fee to the Tribunal is £100.00 and the hearing fee (on receiving notice of a hearing date) is £200.00. These fees are the same as those in relation to a statutory lease extension.

- The Tribunal determination becomes final twenty-one days after it is sent out by the Tribunal. Appeals must be made within this period to the Upper Tribunal with leave of the Tribunal.

- The freeholder must provide a draft contract within twenty-one days of the Tribunal's determination becoming final (taking into account rights of appeal). The parties are expected to enter into the contract within a period of two months after the Tribunal's decision becomes final (the 'appropriate period').

- If the appropriate period elapses without exchanging contracts, then the participating tenants must apply to court within a further two months for a Vesting Order.

Again, the statutory process may seem daunting at first. To most property lawyers it will be as it involves "paperwork" that is for litigators, but I hope that I have set out here that it is nothing actually to be afraid of. Again, the key to any successful legal matter is to make sure that things are done promptly, on time and in the right order. If the procedure set out within the Act is followed, then you should not have any issue.

Please keep in mind that if you serve the initial notice wrongly or fail to have the same drafted correctly then this will be rejected by the freeholder who will look to you for your costs. You will not be able to serve the notice again for twelve months from the date of deemed withdrawal. This is likely to result in angry clients and further costs as the leases within the block will have become shorter in term length, so the value of the freehold is likely to increase accordingly.

The Dolphin Square case

No discussion on collective enfranchisement would be complete without reference to the Dolphin Square case. The full details can be found at Westbrook Dolphin Square Ltd v Friends Life Ltd [2014] EWHC 2433.

This case is the leading authority on enfranchisement and to be honest is worthy of a book alone on the facts that it involved. Dolphin Square itself is a very famous building in London. Often it has had famous residents including many household names including politicians and even the Princess Royal. It's picturesque views and unique architecture have lead it to be used for several media uses over the years including the Beatles and Culture Club filming on the roof top.

Dolphin Square was at one time the largest block of apartments in the world. The head lease and underlease were acquired by the American Westbrook group of companies in 2006 and shortly afterwards it granted sub-underleases of 1,223 of the 1,229 flats in Dolphin Square to 612 companies. These were all special/specific purchase vehicles (SPVs) for the sole purpose of acquiring the freehold.

Westbrook wished to acquire the freehold. It is fair to say that the freeholder wished to resist the same and quite literally threw everything they had at the same to try and prevent the acquisition. Every objection that the law surrounding enfranchisement allows was raised by the freeholders plus some more obscure arguments. I would suggest that any of you that wish to practice or are practicing in dealing with enfranchisement should read the case.

The issues before the Court were:

1. Did the SPVs each have qualifying tenancies, or were they precluded from having them by virtue of their being "associated companies" for the purposes of the statute? Remember that if a leaseholder owns more than two apartments in a block then they lose their right to enfranchisement.

2. In the light of the creation of the scheme put in place by Westbrook (that is to say creating the SPV's) in order to provide an opportunity for enfranchisement which would otherwise not exist, was Westbrook prevented from enfranchising because it was not the intention of Parliament to allow such schemes (because they would circumvent what is said to be the apparent intention of the statute)?

3. Would allowing enfranchisement in the above circumstances infringe Friends Life's rights under the Human Rights Act?

4. Was Friends Life entitled to argue the point that the building contains more than 25% of space occupied for non-residential purposes, in the light of the fact that it did not take that point in its counter-notice?

5. If it could take that point, did the building in fact contain more than 25% of such space? If it did, enfranchisement was not allowed.

6. If enfranchisement was not prevented by the above, was the tenants' notice ineffective because it did not "specify the proposed purchase price" within the meaning of the Act. This raised the following subsequent issues that the Court had to consider being:

   i. Is there an objective test for validity based on an objectively justifiable price in valuation terms?

   ii. Is there a subjective test for validity based on the views of the tenant as to its justifiability in valuation terms?

   iii. If the answer to either of the above questions is 'yes', does the section 13 notice in this case pass the test?

7. If the enfranchisement scheme would otherwise operate against Friends Life, could it claim to be the "victim" of a transfer at an undervalue for the purposes of section 423 of the Insolvency Act 1986, and thereby avoid its consequences? This involves two sub-issues:

   i. Was the grant of the SPV leases a transaction at an undervalue?

   ii. (Even if it was, can Friends Life benefit from the section?

As you can see there was determined resistance from the freeholder to the same. In fact, that is probably an understatement. However, when the value of the freehold was stated as £111.6 million in the initial notice then you can understand why the freeholder was not keen to allow enfranchisement to take place.

Addressing answers to each of the numbered points I have highlighted in order:

1. The Act clearly states that a person who holds more than two leases could not be a qualifying tenant. This was why the 612 SPVs were created. However, the Act also provides that "associated companies" which together hold more than two leases are to be treated as one entity.

The definition of "associated companies" is to be found in s. 1159 and Schedule 6 of the Companies Act 2006 and includes subsidiary companies. Whether a company was a subsidiary depended on how it was controlled but the test "depended on legal rights of control, and not on underlying facts about the relationship". In this case the SPVs were not subsidiary companies in this technical sense.

2. The judge held that "Westbrook group as a whole set up the present structure with a view to being able to enfranchise, and that it was done with an eye to the relevant sections of the Act so that the SPVs were not controlled by any one body. It is a somewhat elaborate and carefully crafted scheme. There is no particular commercial purpose behind this particular scheme; it is done for enfranchisement purposes." The question was whether such a scheme fell afoul of the Act. That was a matter of statutory interpretation. The judge commented:

   "At the heart of Mr Jourdan's submissions is his case that if Parliament had appreciated that this sort of thing could happen it would have legislated to prevent it. That may or may not be so, but that is not determinative of much."

   The Judge held that s.5(5) and s.5(6) of the Act (the specific sections that dealt with this) were narrow and specific provisions. The fact that Parliament had not legislated to avoid other obvious avoidance devices (such as trusts) was indicative and there were no provisions suggestive of a wider anti-avoidance purpose.

3. The simple answer was 'no'. One must admire the creative talents of the freeholder's legal advisors in trying to run this argument.

4. The Act did not define either "non-residential" or

"residential" purposes. Mann J did not formulate a test but held that it was possible for premises to be used for residential purposes without being anyone's home. The term "residence" indicated living, as opposed to office, accommodation, and could encompass lodgings. This point was raised by the freeholders as many of the residents within the block did not necessarily use it as their permanent home. For example, many politicians have had or still do rent an apartment there but do not use it all the time.

5. The definition of "common parts" assumed an ordinary meaning of those words. It was not necessary that the parts should be devoted to purposes as a matter of obligation in the leases; residents did not have to have access to them. Applying those principles, less than 25 per cent of the complex was used for non-residential purposes.

6. The requirement that the s.13 notice should specify the proposed purchase price required that it had to contain a genuine opening offer, not a nominal figure. The Court decided that a genuine opening offer did not have to fall within the range of reasonably justifiable valuations, and the tenant did not have to believe that it would be accepted. However, it had to be bona fide in the sense that a reasonable landlord would see it as a real offer. I think we can all agree that an offer of over one hundred million pounds, even if not to what the freeholder valued the same at, is far from a trivial sum. The Court not surprisingly considered that it was a genuine offer.

7. The freeholder could not claim to be the "victim" of a transfer at an undervalue for the purposes of section 423 of the Insolvency Act 1986 because, even if the sub underleases to the SPVs were transactions at an undervalue there was no link between the transaction being at an undervalue and the

> harm alleged. The harm alleged would have occurred even those transactions had been at an over value. The freeholder therefore failed on this point too.

As you can see from the above, the freeholder failed, and Westbrook succeeded. The point I think that is most relevant from this case (and again I would stress that my summary above does not do the same justice) is that Westbrook succeeded as they had excellent legal advice. Their legal team specifically set up the scheme to make sure that they had covered every issue. Now I am sure that they did not see every point of the defence that Friends Life raised but I am certain that they were prepared for the majority. What is clear is that their legal team achieved for them what they wanted by having a solid knowledge of the law surrounding the same.

In my experience clients generally only approach me in relation to undertaking a lease extension or purchasing the freehold when the leases within a block are short or the freeholder has offered to sell the freehold to them. Sometimes though a leaseholder is just concerned about the way that their building is being run or perhaps the level of services provided by the freeholder or their agent or perhaps more likely the costs being levied under their service charge. An alternative to carrying out a lease extension or purchasing the freehold can be found under the legislation passed that allows leaseholders within a block to take over the right to manage the building themselves. We will look at this in the next chapter.

CHAPTER FIVE

RIGHT TO MANAGE

The Commonhold & Leasehold Reform Act 2002 provides that leaseholders within a block of flats can take over the day-to-day running of the building from the freeholder by forming a Right to Manage company (RTM). The leaseholders can take over all the management functions that the freeholder performs under the lease. The RTM formed can take on all the responsibilities under the lease that the freeholder had including enforcing covenants but crucially they cannot take over the freeholders right to forfeit. As the freeholder retains the freehold itself then if they pass the right to forfeit to the RTM then they run the risk of their asset depreciating unnecessarily.

To qualify to set up an RTM then certain criteria must be passed:

- The right applies to leaseholders of a building or part of a building containing at least two flats.

- At least two-thirds of the flats in the building must be owned by long leaseholders (leases of more than 21 years when first granted).

- At least half of the flats in the building, held by long leaseholders, must take part.

- The building does not qualify for RTM if the non-residential areas, e.g. shops, make up more than 25% of the whole floor area of the building.

- The building may not qualify if there are four or fewer flats and there is a resident landlord.

The criteria are not unlike those explored in the previous statutory provisions we have examined for lease extensions and freehold enfranchisement. I guess the major difference with an RTM is that unlike a lease extension which only affects one leaseholder at a time or collective enfranchisement which affects only those who are purchasing the freehold then the Right to Manage provisions affect all leaseholders. Those who do not participate are still affected by the fact that costs will be charged to them via the service charges they are responsible for under the terms of their leases.

Setting up an RTM

This is relatively straightforward and again I think a Participation Agreement would be of benefit for those who wish to take part would be wise to enter into in the first place. The procedure is as follows:

- The leaseholders who wish to take part must set up an RTM company using prescribed Articles of Association.

- A notice inviting participation must be served on all leaseholders who are not members, or who have not agreed to become members.

- A Notice of claim for RTM must be the served on the freeholder not earlier than two weeks after the above notice. This is a technical notice and, ideally, should be drawn up by a professional.

- The freeholder can challenge the RTM by counter-notice within one month.

If the freeholder does challenge, then the RTM company can apply to the First-tier tribunal (Property Chamber) for a ruling as to whether they have the Right to Manage. If the freeholder does not challenge, the RTM company acquires Right to Manage four months from the date of the notice of claim ("the acquisition date"). The freeholder should provide details to the RTM company of existing contractors and notify those contractors of the takeover by the RTM company. The RTM company does not have to keep the same contractors and in many cases I imagine that is the reason they have originally decided to exercise the right to set up an RTM in the first place.

Once the RTM has been set up it takes over the functions of the freeholder, but they must keep the freeholder informed of all decisions made. For example, any consents to underletting or agreed consensual alterations to any of the leasehold properties. It is worth noting that the freeholder is entitled to apply and become a member of the RTM company after the acquisition date.

The RTM provisions cannot be exercised when a local authority or housing association is the freeholder. This will be no surprise to you given that similar exemptions exist for enfranchisement and lease extensions respectively.

The current landmark case in relation to RTM matters is Ninety *Broomfield Road RTM Co Ltd v Triplerose Ltd [2015] EWCA Civ 282* . This confirmed that he right to manage cannot be exercised by a single RTM company in respect of more than one self-contained building or part of a building.

The upper Tribunal decided that an RTM should be permitted to manage more than building so the freeholder appealed to the Court of Appeal on the following basis:

- The freehold submitted that the purpose of the 2002 Act

was to allow qualifying leaseholders to assume management of their own buildings through the medium of RTM companies. The purpose of the Act was not intended to allow anyone else to do so i.e. only parties in one building should have the benefit.

- The 2002 Act could only be interpreted as meaning there had to be one RTM Company for each exercise of the right to manage; that is, for each block. The provisions of the Act did not permit the concept of "global" RTM companies applying to premises with different geographical footprints.

- The reference to "premises" in the Act had to have the same meaning wherever it was used unless expressly provided otherwise.

- This analysis was supported by

    a. the consultation paper Commonhold and Leasehold Reform CM4438, August 2000 (the consultation paper) which came before the draft bill which ultimately became the Act, and

    b. the practical consequences which would follow if the Upper Tribunal's decision was found to be correct.

The Court of Appeal agreed. Section 71 of the Act states that the right to manage can be acquired only in relation to premises to which the Act applies and by a company which in accordance with the Act may acquire and exercise right to manage.

S72 (1) applies to premises which had to consist of "a self-contained building or part of the building" so making it clear that the acquisition and exercise of rights to manage applies not to several blocks or self-contained buildings in an estate but to a single self-contained building (i.e. structurally detached) or part of a building.

That was not in itself enough to decide the question whether one RTM Company could acquire the right to manage more than one set of premises.

By s74 those entitled to membership of an RTM Company are qualifying tenants of flats contained in the premises and landlords under leases of the whole or any part of the premises.

For example, if a company was an RTM Company in relation to one building (building x), only qualifying tenants of building x and relevant landlords of building x are entitled to be members of that RTM Company.

Section 74 does not envisage that qualifying tenants of flats contained in another adjacent building (building y) and relevant landlords of building y are also entitled to be members of that RTM Company.

The Court made it clear that the Act could have so provided by envisaging or permitting a complex membership structure of RTM companies by which there were different classes of members in relation to different premises in respect of which the RTM Company had acquired the right to manage. However, the Act does not do so.

The court also found that a close look at the regulations and model articles of association of the RTM Company leads an objective view that a single building or set of premises was intended by the Act otherwise provisions of decision making by members and for the appointment of directors by means of an ordinary resolution would be "completely undermined." For instance, most of the qualifying tenants in relation to building x on an estate could outvote the views of the qualifying tenants in relation to building y.

The court went on to review the real practical problems that would come about if a single RTM Company could take over the management of many blocks or separate buildings. For example, it would be possible for the members of the larger block to out vote decisions of the smaller block. Furthermore, there is scope for great conflicts of interest between leaseholders of different blocks on several issues such as service charges, granting approvals, carrying out major works and estate rules and regulations.

However attractive it might seem for a smaller block to join in a single, estate-wide RTM, this would mean that smaller block could not achieve the objective of self-management which defeats the object of the Act in the first place! The acquisition of the right to manage could not be exercised against an existing RTM Company. Therefore, leaseholders in a smaller block would in practice be fixed with the choice of the RTM Company for all time. The only way in practice to change the situation would be to apply to the appropriate tribunal to appoint a manager under Landlord and Tenant Act 1987, Pt. 2. This procedure would be costly and time consuming which naturally smaller blocks of flats would be unlikely to enter into.

Some key phrases from the judgement in my opinion are:

> *"The relevant provisions of the Act, construed, in context, necessarily point to the conclusion that the words "the premises" have the same meaning wherever they are used (save where otherwise expressly provided).*
>
> *"That means that the references in section 72 to "premises" are to a single self-contained building or part of the building, and that likewise references to "the premises" or "premises" or "any premises" in sections 73, 74, 78 79 and other provisions of the Act are likewise references to a single self-contained building or part of the building.*
>
> *"That interpretation is consistent with the provisions for model articles contained in the Regulations and is the only basis upon*

> *which the machinery for acquisition of the right to manage can operate.*
>
> *"Accordingly, in my view it is not open to an RTM Company to acquire the right to manage more than one self-contained building or part of a building and the Upper Tribunal was wrong to reach the decision which it did."*

Faced with an estate comprising multiple buildings then even if it has one freeholder and is managed as one "unit", to embark upon right to manage will involve the creation of a single RTM Company for each building, serving invitation notices on the tenant of each building and ultimately serving a claim notice on the landlord and any relevant third party in respect of each building. Care must be taken to ensure that each building qualifies and that a sufficient number of qualifying tenants are members of the RTM Company before each claim notice is served. This something that you will need to establish early when discussing with your clients. If you have ten potential participants out of say eighteen leasehold properties, then take time to make sure that there are sufficient numbers per block and point out they will need an RTM for each.

The Law Commission published their report into Right to Manage in July 2020. The report looked at all the weaknesses within the same and suggested solutions to the same. The summary itself of the report from the Law Commission is nearly twenty pages long but I think it can be further summarised by saying that their main suggestion is to give the RTM more legal status, standing and power. For instance to allow the RTM to make applications to First Tier Property Tribunal, stopping freeholders being able to charge for consents due under a lease as the RTM should prevent that and perhaps most importantly allowing the RTM to be able to have a legal right to charge for their management costs from leaseholders. All in all the proposals, and keep in mind they are only just proposals, are to strengthen the position of an RTM. All noble ideas but the fact remains that an RTM is not the same as owning the freehold to the block where there are multiple leasehold units.

So, we have looked at all things leasehold. What if I told you that as well as freehold and leasehold there was a third option. Yes, the rarely used but still potentially relevant commonhold form of tenure exists and we will look at that next.

CHAPTER SIX

COMMONHOLD

The joke among a lot of property lawyers is that there are more books and articles on commonhold then there are commonhold properties. Sadly, this is probably true. Accurate numbers are difficult to estimate but there are around one hundred and fifty. There are probably closer to two hundred books (which this adds to I guess).

The Labour led Governments of 1997 to 2010 had a unique advantage to most Governments of the United Kingdom in that it had a large majority which allowed it to push through legislation without too much difficulty. There was a large emphasis on changing the way the house buying process worked, a lot of us will remember the joy of Home Information Packs… Having said this the rival Conservative Party manifestos of the time also suggested that a change was needed in the way that properties were purchased and owned.

For the legal purists Commonhold allowed something unique that freehold titles would not permit. This is the ability to allow positive covenants to be enforced as they can't "run with the land". Commonhold permits this. However as most of you will know from dealing with newly built developments then the imposition of a management company with an annual rent charge negates this perceived defect with freehold and positive covenants.

The Commonhold and Leasehold Reform Act 2002 introduced Commonhold as it is now. Let's look at how it is constructed.

The set up

Commonhold allows the freehold ownership of individual flats, houses and non-residential units within a building or an estate. Ownership is not limited by time as it is with a lease. The rest of the building or estate forming the commonhold is owned and managed jointly by the flat or unit-holders, through a commonhold association.

A commonhold can only be created out of freehold land, or a freehold building, and comes into effect when the land is registered at the Land Registry as a commonhold. A commonhold can be a new building or an existing building or unbuilt land. Once the commonhold is in place, the new law provides a statutory framework of rights and obligations between the owners of each flat (referred to as unit-holders) and between the unit-holders and the commonhold association.

The freehold estate in commonhold land is divided into units and common parts. A unit may be a flat or may have some non-residential use like an office or shop and could include a garage or a parking space. The Land Registry will create a registered title per unit and one for the common parts. You will see this is not that different to having a leasehold title per separate unit with the communal areas either under a head lease or the freehold title to the Estate as a whole.

Each unit-holder owns the freehold of a unit. As a freehold, the unit will not be subject to restrictions on its sale or transfer or be subject to forfeiture (unlike leasehold). However, its use will be governed by the rules of the commonhold.

The common parts are every part of the building that is not contained in a unit, for example, in a commonhold comprising a block of flats, the common parts will include the actual structure – the walls and roof, the lift and the stairs etc, and common areas such as the corridors and entrance hall, the car park etc. The freehold of the common parts is owned by the commonhold association. The unit-holder is entitled to be a member of the commonhold association. Only unit-holders within the commonhold may be members of the association and ownership of the unit provides the entitlement to be a member, although there is a special rule in relation to joint owners.

The commonhold association is a limited company, registered at Companies House. It is run according to its Memorandum & Articles which are available for inspection at both Companies House and the Land Registry. The Memorandum & Articles are prescribed by the regulations and set out the functions of the commonhold association. This is not dissimilar to how an RTM Company operates.

The commonhold association is subject to the provisions of the Commonhold and Leasehold Reform Act 2002, the Commonhold Regulations 2004 and the Commonhold Community Statement (CCS). The CCS will define the extent of each unit and the common parts and the percentages each unit will contribute to the running costs of the building. It will also set out the duties and obligations of the commonhold association and of each unit-holder. This is like the rights and obligations of both freeholder and a leaseholder contained in leases, but the difference is that there will only be one document for the whole building, not one per flat.

The Commonhold Community Statement will be registered along with the commonhold association's title at the Land Registry. The CCS provides for a commonhold association to set a commonhold assessment, the estimate of the overall costs of the general operation of the building, its maintenance, repair and insurance. There may also be one or more reserve funds. The commonhold association will request payment from each unit-holder in accordance with the percentage allocated to each unit in the Commonhold Community

Statement. Although the unit-holder will own a freehold flat, he or she will not have complete freedom to do anything he wishes in the property. Again, this is not unlike the "traditional relationship" between leaseholder and freeholder.

The use and occupation of the flat will be subject to the rules of the Commonhold Community Statement, perhaps relating to letting, alterations and nuisance, like the restrictions more commonly contained in leases. The unit-holder will have the opportunity to actively participate in the decision-making process in the running of the building. In managing the building, the commonhold association will have a role similar to a landlord/freeholder under a lease, but the difference in a commonhold is that the unit-holder will be represented in that association and be able to express a view on management. This will bring responsibilities for each commonholder.

Commonhold is based on ownership and management of the common asset, the building, by the group of unit-holders; as such, each unit-holder should be prepared to be involved in decision making, to attend and vote at meetings of the commonhold association. This principle of self-management means that unit-holders will not need, and do not have, many of the various statutory rights and protections available to leaseholders. I have heard more than once that Commonhold is more of a commune and way of life than a simple case of owning property.

Commonhold unit itself

A commonhold unit is that part of the commonhold which is owned exclusively by the unit-holder on a freehold basis; it can be a house or flat, an office or other commercial use, or a piece of unbuilt land within a commonhold estate.

The unit may include, within its definition, a garage or a parking space situated elsewhere in the commonhold, or these can be units, owned separately. Where the unit is a flat in a block then, as with a leasehold flat, the ownership of a commonhold unit will usually be limited to the wall, ceiling and floor coverings and the space between them, and will not include external walls. In this situation, just like leasehold, the structure of the building, the walls and floors, are not owned as part of the unit but will be included in the common parts, owned by the commonhold association.

The common parts may also include "limited-use areas", which are areas of the common parts where the use is exclusive to a unit-holder or unit-holders, or the use itself is restricted. The purpose of a limited-use area is to be able to include it within the ownership and management responsibility of the commonhold association while still providing a special use to one or more unit-holders or to restrict it to a particular use, no matter who uses it. The most useful example is a balcony to a flat; this is likely to be part of the physical structure of the building and it is sensible to reserve the responsibility for its maintenance and repair to the commonhold association rather than to the unit-holder. This follows how most modern leases grant exclusive easements to use the balcony per apartment rather than including the same within the demise.

A similar arrangement could apply to an allocated car-parking space in a parking area, again just like in more modern leases that avoid including the parking space within the ownership of an apartment. A further limited-use area could be part of the building to which the unitholders would not normally require, or be allowed, access, such as a boiler room or lift motor room, where use will be limited to specified persons, or, perhaps a caretaker's flat or office where use is limited to the caretaker.

As you can see the drafting of the Act did try to think of everything.

The Commonhold Community Statement

For some reason I always think of this as some sort of political philosophy.

The CCS is the central and most important document in the commonhold; it forms the rules governing how the commonhold is used and managed. In a commonhold, the unit-holders are required to contribute financially to the whole and are bound by restrictions and obligations in the use of their unit and the common parts, through the CCS.

In simple terms, the CCS provides the rules and guidance to manage the building or estate and to regulate the rights and duties of the commonhold community, through one single, common document. (The Mem & Arts govern the operation of the company, the commonhold association; the CCS governs the operation of the commonhold itself, the building or estate. Both documents are subject to the Commonhold Regulations).

The CCS

- Identifies the units (by listing them);
- Confirms the number of Units;
- Identifies the common parts;
- Confirms all the above by reference to a plan;
- Sets out the percentage to each unit in respect of the commonhold assessment – the proportion the unit contributes to the overall running costs of the commonhold;
- Sets out the percentage to each unit in respect of any

separate levy for a reserve fund;

- Allocates the number of votes to each unit;
- Sets the rules for the running of the commonhold.

The form and most of the content of the CCS is prescribed and every CCS must include all the provisions in the prescribed document.

A commonhold association can add extra provisions relevant to the individual commonhold but may not amend or delete any prescribed provision; any extra provisions must be clearly indicated by a heading which includes the words 'additional provisions specific to this commonhold' and set out at the end of the relevant section or part of the CCS or as an annex to the CCS.

The provisions will not be effective until they are registered at the Land Registry. The CCS is registered at the Land Registry along with the title documents for the commonhold and therefore fully accessible to present and potential unit-holders. It is a document which creates legally binding rights and duties; the ownership of a commonhold unit is subject to rights, obligations and duties on both the unit-holder, any tenants of a unit and the commonhold association as set out in the CCS. The closest comparison is with a lease – acquisition of a leasehold flat is subject to the rights and obligations of the lease. In a commonhold there are no separate leases for each flat; the CCS is a single document applicable to all units in the commonhold. The CCS must contain the following information; definition of the commonhold: the CCS will include a plan, or plans, to show the overall extent of the commonhold and the location and extent of each commonhold unit, the common parts and any limited-use areas. It will state the number of units and the rights of passage and access reserved both to and over the units and the common parts. Having the same registered with the Land

Registry is a good idea as it means that a copy is readily available (in theory) but I imagine that any changes will of course mean updating the same at the Land Registry.

The CCS will, in this way, be like a lease in that it defines the unit and the rights it both benefits from and is subject to, for example, the rights of access to the unit through the common parts but also the obligations to allow access to the unit by the commonhold association in certain circumstances. The plan will need to comply with the requirements of the Land Registry (The Commonhold Community Statement (CCS).

Commonhold allocations set out the percentage the unit must contribute as its share of the overall costs of the commonhold and any reserve fund. The CCS sets the percentages allocated to each unit which must total one hundred. Therefore, every present and prospective unit-holder is aware of the relative contributions. The CCS also allocates the number of votes the unit-holder will be able to exercise in a poll/vote when take. This may be based on an equal vote per unit but may instead reflect the relative size of each unit, on the basis that a larger unit making a greater contribution to the commonhold assessment should be entitled to a proportionately larger vote in the management of the building. I can see that this could cause issues in the future. Using an analogy of various Tribunal decisions on service charges, the ground floor apartments in a block of leasehold apartments with a lift system have often argued they should pay less than those that live on the floors above them. Allocating voting rights depending on size is another one of those arguments waiting to happen as all will still use the same communal space you would think.

The rules within the CCS include specific provision for repairing, maintenance and insuring obligations of the commonhold association. The commonhold association must produce an annual estimate of the income required from the unit-holders to maintain, insure, manage and repair the building to which each unit-holder is required to contribute according to the percentage allocated to the unit, upon notice from the association.

The CCS requires that the directors of the commonhold association must, during the first year in which the commonhold is registered, formally consider the commissioning of a reserve study from a suitable professional and must, in any event, carry out such a study at least once in every ten years. The directors may decide to establish a reserve fund or funds or the members, the unit-holders, may by resolution require them to do so. The CCS then enables the association to set a levy and to require payment on notice to the unit holders. If the property is rented out then the unit holder can be directed that the tenant in the unit should divert their rent equivalent to the levy to the association (this will comply with the tenant's contractual requirements for proper payment of rent to his landlord, the unit-holder).

Although a residential unit may be let by the unit-holder, this cannot include the grant of a lease of the unit at a premium or for a term of more than seven years. This is to prevent the creation of long residential leases within the commonhold. Non-residential units are not subject to this restriction on leasing. A commercial unit can be leased in the traditional way on this basis.

The CCS allows for special rights and obligations specific to the commonhold. They may be added throughout the CCS but only in the manner permitted by the regulations. There is a particular annex which must include the rate of interest to be applied to late payments (if any), the permitted uses of the units and the common parts, the details of insured risks and the authorised uses and users of the limited-use areas. This annex is prescribed in form but not in content and the association will draft the necessary rules.

On new Estates in some cases the developer may wish to reserve rights for future development of the land or the commonhold.

These rights will be limited in time and will cease once the developer has completed the building works and sold the last unit. Any such rights will be contained in a final annex of the CCS. Within the prescribed structure of the CCS it will be possible to make amendments, for example, to the extent of individual units or to rights over common parts, or changes to local rules. The procedure for making changes will be subject to the rules of the CCS but all amendments to the CCS must be registered at the Land Registry and do not apply until the amended CCS is registered.

Having looked at all of this then I expect you will consider this to be a well thought out logical piece of legislation. Why then are there not more Commonholds? Ask yourself, how many have you dealt with?

Commonhold – the flaws?

Advocates of Commonhold have argued on occasion that the reason that the tenure has not "caught on" is because of the economic recession that affected the country around it's time of launch. To be fair Commonhold was available before the "credit crunch" so I think those that argue that have a weak framework.

In reality there is no desire for the same. Developers have not shown any interest in Commonhold. The few Commonholds that are in existence tend to be in relation to retirement properties. The commercial reality is that if a developer can build a large block of apartments which are sold on a leasehold basis then they can sell the freehold for rates often more than thirty times the combined ground rent receipts per annum. With sums of several hundred thousands of pounds sometimes changing hands for the freehold to a block of apartments why would developers (who exist to make profit) consider Commonhold?

Perhaps more importantly is the resistance of the financial

institutions who make up the clear majority of residential mortgage lenders in the UK having an indifference to Commonhold. Advocates of Commonhold have tried to persuade developers that they can sell Commonhold units at a premium as they will be freehold as opposed to leasehold. There is often a perception in those outside the property industry that freehold is best. However, if a mortgage lender is not prepared to loan monies against a Commonhold then that argument is negated completely. Yes, lenders may have criteria that need to be met in relation to the terms of a long residential lease but most mortgages available to residential buyers are not available for Commonhold.

Whilst the option remains that leasehold owners of apartments could agree to convert to Commonhold this is not easy to do. Unlike the rights of enfranchisement and the Right to Manage, options to convert to Commonhold would be cumbersome to say the least. A simple majority for starters is not enough to apply for this, it requires all leaseholders to agree so practically would be very difficult.

In addition to the legislation which allows for lease extension, enfranchisement and the Right to Manage being in place, the rights of leaseholders have been greatly improved. It is much easier to challenge service charge demands for instance than it has been in the past. Dare I say that Commonhold as it is currently set up is more of a "lifestyle choice". Many clients who approach you regarding a lease extension or enfranchisement are probably doing so because of necessity (wanting to sell or reduce service charge or perceived poor block management) rather than wanting to form a community where they live. I know I am a cynic.

A couple of things strike me from the setting up of the CCS. The restrictions over the granting of long leases of a residential commonhold unit mean that a lease cannot be granted for a premium for a lease longer than 7 years. This is clearly to prevent the reintroduction of residential long leases into the commonhold system.

However, it ignores the need for shared ownership leases which are often a key component of new housing developments. Shared ownership could be a driving force for the introduction of Commonhold if the legislation was amended. It could mean a hybrid form of commonhold, but this might encourage the growth of the same. No such leasing restrictions exist over non-residential commonhold units so there is a precedent for the removal within other parts of the legislation.

The second issue relates to dispute settlement. When considering Commonhold one of the progressive points of it is the use of mediation to solve disputes along with the standardisation of commonhold rules. With certain important exceptions (unlawful use of the commonhold unit or non-payment of the commonhold assessments etc) disputes must be referred to mediation. The Act provides for the appointment of a Commonhold Ombudsman. You won't be surprised that due to the low number of Commonhold units this has not been set up. If it were then this could resolve matters amicably.

However, on this point I have to say that in my experience that when monies need to be demanded from a "neighbour" then often said neighbour finds it easy to ignore such requests. When you must see someone every day it can be difficult to ask for what is rightfully owed. A threatening letter from a third-party managing agent often has more effect.

Is Commonhold the future?

My response is that it could be. The current Government and media appear to be keen to try and rectify what they perceive to be weakness in the leasehold framework that we have in place for residential properties. The Commonhold legislation will have to be looked at again though with the flaws above addressed. In addition, there needs to be some impetus to encourage developers and perhaps more importantly financial institutions to accept this form of legal tenure.

If the changes coupled with some impetus from Government and others is forthcoming, then we may see more Commonhold developments. Let's face it, currently you are more likely to find hen's teeth than be working on a Commonhold file on your desk.

Currently the media seem very keen on the concept of Commonhold, without fully understanding the same, because of the perceived "leasehold scandal" involving the charging of ground rents on leaseshold houses on various more modern sites of properties by several large national property developers. In July 2020 the Law Commission published their latest report on Commonhold. There were several interesting points made from the same but I think the most interesting one was the open letter they wrote to Mortgage Lenders.

I have used the word "indifference" earlier in this chapter to describe lenders collective stance on Commonhold. I think outright rejection of the same would actually be a better description. Lenders will on the whole not lend on Commonhold. Lenders acceptance of the same is key. I recall watching a wonderful TV program that shall remain nameless but it involves successful business folk named after a mythical creature that breathes fire being asked to invest in various companies presented before them for a percentage of the ownership of the company or product before them. One involved the use of straw to build new homes. No one of the three pigs was not involved.

The business people sat in their leather chairs were literally wowed by the same. It was cheaper than traditional methods of construction and around 30% more energy efficient. The same were prefabricated and could be built very quickly. They were all raving about the same until some asked what mortgage lenders thought of the same. Lenders would not lend against the same. Chances of investment were over.

Lenders acceptance is key. The open letter that I refer to from the Law Commission to lenders made various suggestions to entice their acceptance to the same. These included:

- Allowing lenders to be able to make applications to the First Tier Property Tribunal if the Directors of the Commonhold were not acting to comply with the obligations imposed on them under the commonhold community statement. Such standing is not offered to lenders with leasehold properties.

- Lenders have most concern I believe over the fact that if the commonhold association becomes insolvent they are left with a property that is a flying freehold. As you are probably aware lenders do not like flying freeholds. The fact that there is a whole section in the UK Finance Lenders Handbook dedicated to the situation regarding flying freeholds (5.7 for those who did not know) which tells you how seriously they take the same. The Law Commission suggests that public liability insurance, making a reserve fund compulsory for a commonhold association and having a better procedure in place for those not paying towards the commonhold costs to reclaim monies owed will all encourage lenders to provide mortgages against commonhold units.

Sadly I am still not convinced. In reality lenders are very conservative with a small "c" and lending against something as "exotic" as commonhold I do not forsee in the near future. Given that compulsory registration of land only really took place sixty years after the creation of the Law of Property Act 1925, mainly due to mortgage lenders (and lawyers) hostility to the same I am not seeing commonhold as the panacea that some commentators make it out to be.

So, having looked at the options for leaseholders to potentially deal with unscrupulous landlords/freeholders then I think it is about time to consider matters from the "other side of the fence". In the next chapter I will recap the matters discussed in the previous chapters but with a view from acting for the freeholder/landlord.

CHAPTER SEVEN

ACTING FOR THE FREEHOLDER

This work can be very lucrative. Collecting unpaid ground rent, collecting unpaid service charges, dealing with the enforcement/breach of leasehold restrictive covenants and assisting with the day-to-day legal work of a commercial landlord with their blocks of apartments to which they own the freehold is a good source of work. Get it wrong though and that work can just as soon disappear. In this chapter we will review the issues discussed in the previous chapters to see how you should be advising the freeholder including hopefully some tips you can pass on to them.

Lease extensions

Commercial freeholders are not always that keen for lease extensions to take place. Now there is no denying that they will obtain a premium for granting the same, but they will be reluctant to do so. Firstly, once they have granted one lease extension in a block then others are likely to follow so they don't necessarily want to make it to easy for fear of others following suit. Secondly the premium for a lease extension is often not the primary purpose of owning the freehold as they make monies from the long-term maintenance etc.

Keeping this all in mind then it is vital that when you are advising your freeholder client that you are conversant with the law surrounding the same. More importantly the nuances around the same.

Your client may wish to not grant a lease extension willingly, so it will be for you to check the notices served to see if they are correct. There are many things to consider. To try and help you I have listed some things for you to consider below but please keep in mind that this is far from an exhaustive list:

- Does the leaseholder meet the criteria to serve a Section 42 notice?

- Have they failed to serve notice on an intermediate landlord?

- Is the valuation realistic? You may not be a valuer but you will be able to advise your client that it needs to be.

- Have they provided all the information you need to advise your client? If not remember you have only twenty-one days to request the same.

- Remember you need to respond within twenty-one days of the date specified in the notice.

- If the respective surveyors cannot agree on a figure, then you can advise your client to proceed to Tribunal.

- Even if the Tribunal decision (assume it goes that far) is not to the satisfaction of your client then remind them that they have a right of appeal.

- Remember that a draft lease must be with the leaseholders' solicitors within fourteen days of any Tribunal decision.

- Also remember that you have two months after the decision to agree the terms of the new lease. If the leaseholder fails to do this, perhaps because they need to raise finance to pay the agreed premium which may not be in place, then you can apply for the agreement to be nullified

The statutory process is very specific in what must be contained within the terms of a lease extension as we examined earlier in the book (90-year extension to the term with peppercorn ground rent etc). However just because your client has received a notice this does not preclude them for making an offer of a lease extension that is not on statutory terms. Again, as I have referred to earlier it is perfectly possible to agree terms agreeable to all parties on a non-statutory basis.

If your client proceeds on a voluntary basis then they can always use this to obtain far more favourable terms than those on offer from statutory terms. For example, your client could retain the right to be paid ground rent or amend other terms in their favour. Often, I have seen that freeholder's solicitors look for the right to be added to the lease to charge interest for late payments as quite often these are not specifically stated within a lease.

Keep in mind that most people that wish to have a lease extension are doing so because they must, not because they want to. Whether this be due to the fact their lease is too short to attractive buyers at a decent value or they cannot raise finance against the property without the lease term being extended they are keen to extend.

It would be worth bringing this to your client's attention. A lease extension for instance does not have to be for a long period of time. It is possible to offer a shorter extension to allow the leaseholder what they desire. For instance, you could offer an extension of say only twenty-five years. This would attract a smaller premium for the leaseholder who if they are selling may find more attractive. Twenty-five years seems like a long time (it is the length of most initial residential mortgage terms) but it is not.

For instance, if the lease to be extended only has seventy full years remaining at the time of extension then a lease extension of twenty-five years will increase the term to ninety-five years. Five years after extension then when the term is within eighty years remaining then a prudent solicitor is likely to advise anyone involved with ownership of said leasehold property to be looking at extending the lease. By offering a shorter term for any lease extension then you will be offering your client to have the benefit of more favourable lease terms with the clear opportunity for a further premium to be charged for in the future.

As I have said this is not an exhaustive list but all points that require consideration if you are advising the freeholder on matters.

Right of First Refusal

Before looking at matters from the perspective of advising a freeholder client who does not want to sell you may be instructed by those who don't want to have ownership of a freehold block. There could be lots of reasons why a freeholder may wish to sell, a developer who does not want to retain the ownership of a freehold to a block of flats following the leasehold sales, wishing to "cash in" their asset or simply that they no longer wish to have the issues surrounding with owning a freehold.

So, if your freeholder client instructs you to deal with the legal side of disposing of the freehold what should you do first?

Firstly, you need to establish whether notice must be served on the leasehold owners within the block before considering any sale. The law provides that the "Right of First Refusal" to purchase a freehold when being sold may have to be offered to the leaseholders within the block in question first.

The Landlord & Tenant Act 1987 (as amended) can give the leaseholders, and some tenants, of a building the Right of First

Refusal (RFR) when the Landlord is selling the freehold. The right is not an individual right to buy the freehold attributed to each leaseholder, but a collective right in respect of the whole building.

The right of first refusal (RFR) only applies if the building qualifies. For the building to qualify (just as in enfranchisement):

- It must contain at least two flats

- No more than 50% of the building should be in non-residential use (based on floor area excluding common parts)

- More than 50% of the flats in the building must be held by "qualifying tenants" (put simply again long leaseholders fixed or periodic tenancies, other than assured shorthold tenancies) Someone who is a leaseholder of three or more flats in the building will not be a qualifying tenant.

If the building qualifies, the obligation on the Landlord to give the leaseholders RFR only applies when there is a "relevant disposal".

Most sales will trigger RFR, the most common being a straight-forward sale of the freehold. There are several exceptions which will not trigger RFR such as the following:

- Grant of single tenancies. The disposal must apply to the whole building so the Landlord is free to grant tenancies /leases of individual flats.

- Disposal to an associated company. This is where the Landlord disposes of his interest to another company which has been associated with the parent company for at least two years.

- Disposal to certain relatives of the freeholder if it is within an individual's name.

- Disposals arising from leaseholders exercising their right to buy the freehold under the Leasehold Reform, Housing and Urban Development Act 1993. Obvious but worth stating.

The offer of RFR is to be given to each individual qualifying tenant by the Landlord by means of section 5 notice. To accept the offer more than fifty percent of the qualifying tenants must accept the offer, jointly, within 2 months of the notice.

The observant amongst you will note that the percentage of qualifying tenants is different to that required under the 1993 Act, which only requires 50% to make a claim.

It is important to appreciate the following

- It is an opportunity for the tenants to purchase that interest before it is offered on the open market or by auction. This is not the same as enfranchisement.

- The right follows your client's decision to sell and the leaseholder can only react to your client's offer. Your client can withdraw the offer at any time before the contract is binding.

- The right is available both to leaseholders and regulated (fair rent) tenants but not to houses occupied as single dwellings.

- The price is set by your client, or by auction where the landlord decides to sell that way. There is no right for that price to be determined by a First-tier Tribunal (Property Chamber) or anyone else. However, you need to make it clear to your client that they cannot sell or offer the interest to another party on different terms or at a lower price than that originally offered within twelve months of their notice, unless they again offer the right to the existing tenants on the new terms and/or at the lower figure.

- The right is not available to tenants of local authorities and housing associations. In the unlikely event that the freeholder lives in the building then it may not be available then either.

Serving the notice

The requirement to make the offer and the procedure involved is set out in the Act. If a landlord fails to comply with any of these statutory requirements he commits a criminal offence. Therefore, this is a serious matter as failure to comply correctly could leave your client with a criminal record. The criteria also apply where the landlord's interest is being sold by a Receiver, a Trustee in bankruptcy or an Executor following grant of probate.

So, what to do?

Well you need to serve the notice. Believe it or not there are five different notices that you can use. They are:

Section 5A	sale by private contract
Section 5B	sale by public auction
Section 5C	a grant of an option or right of pre-emption
Section 5D	sale not pursuant to a contract
Section 5E	sale for a non-monetary consideration

In reality you are only likely to come across 5A and 5B notices. Both are basically the same save a few quirks regarding timings which I will list below.

The law requires the freeholder to serve the notice on the qualifying tenants and that is what they (in most cases you) are expected to do. If for some reason the freeholder does not serve notices on everyone (I would suggest it would be foolish not to do so) then you can be considered to have served a valid notice provided not less than 90% of the qualifying tenants have received the same.

If the notice is served on different tenants at different times, resulting in the period for accepting the offer being different, the notice is presumed to have effect for all the tenants as if it provided for the acceptance period to end with the date in the last notice served. I would therefore suggest it is imperative that you serve notice on all of them at the same time so not as to elongate the process.

Be mindful that when a Right to Manage company is in place then a copy of the notice also needs to be served on the Company itself.

Once the notice has been served then your client freeholder cannot sell their interest to anyone other than the tenants until the notice itself has expired.

Section 5A – sale by private contract on the open market

When your freehold client intends to sell on the open market, the notice must include the following:

1. the terms of the proposed disposal, which are the property and the interest being disposed of (the freehold, a headlease etc), the price and any deposit required;

2. a statement that the notice constitutes an offer by the freeholder to enter into a contract on the terms set out in the notice;

3. the date by which the offer may be accepted (the initial period) – this must not be less than two months from the date of the notice; and

4. a date for the nomination by the tenants of a purchaser (the nominated person), which must not be less than a further two months.

Although the procedures appear simple and provide what most consider to be generous time frames for the tenants, there are certain limitations which must be considered:

- The price in the Offer Notice – this is the price set by your client and is not negotiable (unless the freeholder is prepared to enter into discussions regarding the same). It cannot be challenged at a First-tier Tribunal. It is a 'one time" offer, based by the freeholder on what they reasonably expect to achieve in an open market sale. The protection for the tenants is the prohibition on sales within twelve months on different terms or at a lower price – this should prevent the freeholder from setting an unachievably high price to the tenants.

- The requisite majority – the necessary majority of qualifying tenants must be maintained throughout the process; should it drop below the required number the nominated person must advise the freeholder and the tenants must withdraw. The freeholder is then free to sell (but still not at a lower price or on better terms within twelve months). It would therefore be prudent I think to check with the nominated purchaser's solicitor throughout the process that the majority remains.

- Either party may withdraw – the freeholder may withdraw the offer and the nominated person may withdraw their intention to proceed with the transaction at any time up to exchange of contracts; neither is bound to proceed.

- Either party may be deemed to have withdrawn – if the freeholder does not send or exchange contracts the freeholder cannot dispose of the interest for twelve months following deemed withdrawal, or if the nominated person does not return the signed contract they are considered to have withdrawn. If that happens then the freeholder may dispose of his interest during the twelve months following withdrawal but subject to conditions.

- The cost of withdrawal or deemed withdrawal – if a notice of withdrawal is served after the first four weeks of the nomination period specified in the Offer Notice, or if a party is deemed to have withdrawn after this period, the withdrawing party will be liable for the other side's costs. Withdrawal within the first four weeks means that there is no liability for costs. Please keep this in mind when advising your client.

Section 5B – where the landlord intends to dispose by auction.

Selling of a freehold by way of auction can be a very enticing method for a lot of freeholders who wish to sell. They are in with a chance of finding a buyer who will complete as once the "gavel has fallen" at auction then any buyer is exchanged and committed with a deposit to the transaction. It can also help to inflate the price. The process in giving notice to the tenants within the building in question is not that unlike that for those sold by private contract.

The main differences surround the timings.

When your client freeholder wishes to sell at auction, the notice must be served between four and six months before the date of the auction.

The notice must include the following:

1. the principal terms of the proposed disposal, the property and the interest. However, there will be no price or deposit mentioned (the freeholder is not required to divulge the reserve price);

2. that the disposal is to be by public auction;

3. that the notice is an offer by the freeholder for the contract (if any) entered into by the landlord at the auction with the purchaser, to have effect as if the nominated person had entered into it;

4. the initial period for acceptance of at least two months. This initial period must end at least two months before the date of the auction; and

5. a further period of twenty-eight days for the nomination of a purchaser (this is different to a section 5a notice that requires two month). This period must end at least 28 days before the date of the auction.

6. The S5B notice is not required to state the date of the auction, although it would be reasonable to do so. If the date is not included then, at least twenty-eight days before the auction the freeholder must serve a further notice on the requisite majority (not all the qualifying tenants), stating the date, time and place of the auction. For ease I have always tended to state the date of the auction in a side letter that

accompanies the initial notice to the tenants to save having to remember to do so later. This is not essential, but it saves you having to remember to do so later and possibly overlooking the provision which could lead to a challenge from the tenants.

7. If the qualifying tenants wish to accept the offer the requisite majority must do so within the initial period set in your client's notice (unless they agree to a longer period).

8. They must then notify the freehold of their nominated person (most likely you) within the twenty-eight-day further period.

9. The nominated person must send a notice to the freeholder at least twenty eight days before the date of the auction, electing that the remaining stages of the procedure should apply.
   This is different from other provisions in that the tenants cannot rely on the procedure continuing, they must formally advise the landlord that they wish it to do so; failure to serve this notice will result in the tenants' previous acceptance being deemed withdrawn. You should make sure that you have this notice before assuming that the tenants want to go ahead so you can advise your client accordingly. You will also need to advise the auction house as well purely from a practical point of view.

10. The freehold is offered at the auction. The tenants are free to attend or not – they are not required to. Similarly, they are not required to make a bid and would be unwise to do so as this will have the effect of driving up the price – your client may be happy if they did! If a successful bid is accepted at the auction the freeholder must send a copy of the contract to the nominated person within seven days of the auction.

11. The nominated person then has a period of twenty-eight days in which to accept the contract and pay any deposit required. This has the effect of the nominated person and not the successful bidder entering into the contract.

Although the procedures are simple and provide decent time scale for the tenants to action matters, there are certain items which you should make sure you advise your client upon:

- the price is set by the auction and cannot be challenged unless your client is prepared to negotiate. Again, it is a 'take it or leave it' offer but this time at a figure achieved in an open sale.

- if your client withdraws the freehold from the auction, or it does not sell, then the interest cannot be sold, by auction or otherwise, without starting the whole procedure afresh with service of a new S5A or S5B notice. You need to make sure your client is aware of this.

- if the qualifying tenants do not accept the offer made by your freeholder client or notify the nominated person, or if the nominated person withdraws from the acquisition or is deemed to have withdrawn because of a failure to adhere to the time limits, then the freeholder is free to sell at auction within the next twelve months, with no further reference to the tenants, but subject to conditions. However, they may not sell privately (other than a sale at a public auction) without a new notice under S5A, or they commit a criminal offence.

- the nominated person must withdraw if there are no longer sufficient tenants to form a requisite majority. As I have said earlier – watch out for this.

- the nominated person is deemed to have withdrawn where they fail to accept the contract or pay the deposit

- if either party withdraws, or is deemed to have withdrawn, they will be liable for costs.

The S5A and S5B procedures are the most commonly used and the remaining provisions are relatively rare.

Enfranchisement for the freeholder

Sometimes your client will not want to sell. Why would they? This is often their source of income. If your client is presented with a notice requesting enfranchisement then the law is very much drafted in favour of the tenants, provided they do things correctly. Your ability to know the process and the major intricacies of the same could help you to assist your freeholder client to end or at the very least postpone their loss of the freehold to the tenants. In theory as time passes the freehold will become more valuable so please keep this in mind always.

I do not consider the following to be an exhaustive list, but I would suggest that when your freeholder client has received an enfranchisement notice you should be looking at the following:

- Making your client aware that if the tenants withdraw once they have served the notice then your client can look to all the participating tenants for their costs incurred

- Urge your client to obtain expert valuation advice

- Check that the building in question can meet the criteria for enfranchisement

- Check that the tenants participating meet the criteria to be considered "qualifying tenants"

- Make sure you reply to a counter notice in time to avoid a vesting order!

- Check that the tenants have complied with all the time frames

It is worth mentioning to your client that a determined set of tenants will eventually be able to pursue enfranchisement as the law is very much on their side. Often the best advice is to make sure that your client has secured the best price for their asset.

Right to manage for the freeholder

Whilst this may not be to the taste of some freeholders some actively like the concept of the same. Some freeholders won't like the idea that they will no longer have as much control over expenditure on their asset or the chance to earn revenue from repairs, but some may like the idea that they will no longer have to be concerned about the "minutiae" day to day issues – the advantage to a freeholder with a Right to Manage company assuming the management of the building allows the freeholder to sit back. They will still benefit from the ground rent, any lease extensions and any monies they make from insuring the building.

When advising your freeholder client in relation to a Right to Manage situation remind them that they should take their share in the Right to Manage company that is formed. This will allow them to have a say in how the management of the building is handled. I have had clients who are freeholders who have experienced a Right to Manage company that has not worked out for the leaseholders. The leaseholders have all fallen out and management has not taken place. These clients have been welcomed back with open arms by the leaseholders when the Right to Manage company has been dissolved and the freeholder has had to take matters in hand.

Summing up acting for the freeholder

If you are aware of the framework for each area of law as set out in this book, then you can advise your freeholder client with the basics on how to deal with each matter. I would always stress to a freeholder client that they need to be aware that the law allows leaseholders to ask for a lease extension or enfranchisement and the like. Provided they accept that these rights are enshrined in statute then the best way to advise is to make sure that the leaseholders that exercise said rights stick to the procedures. Being able to spot that procedure has not been followed will give you the inevitable satisfaction of being able to advise your client that the leaseholders solicitors have made an error whilst elongating the process which should in theory extend your client's ability to benefit financially.

CHAPTER EIGHT

CONCLUSION

I hope that you have all found the previous chapters of use. The law surrounding these topics is very complex. The same is also somewhat in a state of flux or at least appears that it may be. The aim of this book is to introduce you to the basics of the same. There are numerous cases on each section of the process (serving notice on the freeholder for instance) that could be considered in some depth.

The purpose as I have said is to introduce you to the process involved. I would not consider anyone who has read this book to then consider themselves an expert. As with just about all things in life, dealing with matters first hand is the best way to learn how to do something. A textbook can only take you so far. Like driving, one can learn to pass the test but in reality the only way you really learn is spending time out on the road.

I would suggest that you keep this book handy for reference before you see a client on one of the matters discussed so you are familiar with the processes. Keep in mind that if you follow the procedure for each area you won't go far wrong. Timing as they say is everything. The law is constantly evolving particularly with these areas as you can see from the most recent proposed legislation that I have touched upon.

Thanks for reading and good luck.

MORE BOOKS BY LAW BRIEF PUBLISHING

A selection of our other titles available now:-

'A Practical Guide to Transgender Law' by Robin Moira White & Nicola Newbegin
'Artificial Intelligence – The Practical Legal Issues (2nd Edition)' by John Buyers
'A Practical Guide to Challenging Sham Marriage Allegations in Immigration Law' by Priya Solanki
'A Practical Guide to New Build Conveyancing' by Paul Sams & Rebecca East
'A Practical Guide to Inherited Wealth on Divorce' by Hayley Trim
'A Practical Guide to Shareholder Disputes in Family Businesses' by Ed Weeks
'A Practical Guide to the Law of Forests in Scotland' by Philip Buchan
'A Practical Guide to Health and Medical Cases in Immigration Law' by Rebecca Chapman & Miranda Butler
'A Practical Guide to Bad Character Evidence for Criminal Practitioners by Aparna Rao
'A Practical Guide to Environmental Enforcement' by Christopher Badger & Stuart Jessop
'A Practical Guide to Hoarding and Mental Health for Housing Lawyers' by Rachel Coyle
'A Practical Guide to Psychiatric Claims in Personal Injury – 2nd Edition' by Liam Ryan
'Stephens on Contractual Indemnities' by Richard Stephens
'A Practical Guide to the EU Succession Regulation' by Richard Frimston
'A Practical Guide to Solicitor and Client Costs – 2nd Edition' by Robin Dunne
'Constructive Dismissal – Practice Pointers and Principles' by Benjimin Burgher
'A Practical Guide to Religion and Belief Discrimination Claims in the Workplace' by Kashif Ali
'A Practical Guide to the Law of Medical Treatment Decisions' by Ben Troke

'Fundamental Dishonesty and QOCS in Personal Injury Proceedings: Law and Practice' by Jake Rowley

'A Practical Guide to the Law in Relation to School Exclusions' by Charlotte Hadfield & Alice de Coverley

'A Practical Guide to Divorce for the Silver Separators' by Karin Walker

'The Right to be Forgotten – The Law and Practical Issues' by Melissa Stock

'A Practical Guide to Planning Law and Rights of Way in National Parks, the Broads and AONBs' by James Maurici QC, James Neill et al

'A Practical Guide to Election Law' by Tom Tabori

'A Practical Guide to the Law in Relation to Surrogacy' by Andrew Powell

'A Practical Guide to Claims Arising from Fatal Accidents – 2nd Edition' by James Patience

'A Practical Guide to the Ownership of Employee Inventions – From Entitlement to Compensation' by James Tumbridge & Ashley Roughton

'A Practical Guide to Asbestos Claims' by Jonathan Owen & Gareth McAloon

'A Practical Guide to Stamp Duty Land Tax in England and Northern Ireland' by Suzanne O'Hara

'A Practical Guide to the Law of Farming Partnerships' by Philip Whitcomb

'Covid-19, Homeworking and the Law – The Essential Guide to Employment and GDPR Issues' by Forbes Solicitors

'Covid-19, Force Majeure and Frustration of Contracts – The Essential Guide' by Keith Markham

'Covid-19 and Criminal Law – The Essential Guide' by Ramya Nagesh

'Covid-19 and Family Law in England and Wales – The Essential Guide' by Safda Mahmood

'A Practical Guide to the Law of Unlawful Eviction and Harassment – 2nd Edition' by Stephanie Lovegrove

'Covid-19, Residential Property, Equity Release and Enfranchisement – The Essential Guide' by Paul Sams and Louise Uphill

'Covid-19, Brexit and the Law of Commercial Leases – The Essential Guide' by Mark Shelton

'A Practical Guide to Costs in Personal Injury Claims – 2nd Edition' by Matthew Hoe

'A Practical Guide to the General Data Protection Regulation (GDPR) – 2nd Edition' by Keith Markham

'Ellis on Credit Hire – Sixth Edition' by Aidan Ellis & Tim Kevan

'A Practical Guide to Working with Litigants in Person and McKenzie Friends in Family Cases' by Stuart Barlow

'Protecting Unregistered Brands: A Practical Guide to the Law of Passing Off' by Lorna Brazell

'A Practical Guide to Secondary Liability and Joint Enterprise Post-Jogee' by Joanne Cecil & James Mehigan

'A Practical Guide to the Pre-Action RTA Claims Protocol for Personal Injury Lawyers' by Antonia Ford

'A Practical Guide to Neighbour Disputes and the Law' by Alexander Walsh

'A Practical Guide to Forfeiture of Leases' by Mark Shelton

'A Practical Guide to Coercive Control for Legal Practitioners and Victims' by Rachel Horman

'A Practical Guide to Rights Over Airspace and Subsoil' by Daniel Gatty

'Tackling Disclosure in the Criminal Courts – A Practitioner's Guide' by Narita Bahra QC & Don Ramble

'A Practical Guide to the Law of Driverless Cars – Second Edition' by Alex Glassbrook, Emma Northey & Scarlett Milligan

'A Practical Guide to TOLATA Claims' by Greg Williams

'A Practical Guide to Elderly Law – 2nd Edition' by Justin Patten

'A Practical Guide to the Law of Prescription in Scotland' by Andrew Foyle

'A Practical Guide to the Construction and Rectification of Wills and Trust Instruments' by Edward Hewitt

'A Practical Guide to the Law of Bullying and Harassment in the Workplace' by Philip Hyland

'How to Be a Freelance Solicitor: A Practical Guide to the SRA-Regulated Freelance Solicitor Model' by Paul Bennett

'A Practical Guide to Prison Injury Claims' by Malcolm Johnson

'A Practical Guide to the Small Claims Track – 2nd Edition' by Dominic Bright

'A Practical Guide to Advising Clients at the Police Station' by Colin Stephen McKeown-Beaumont

'A Practical Guide to Antisocial Behaviour Injunctions' by Iain Wightwick
'Practical Mediation: A Guide for Mediators, Advocates, Advisers, Lawyers, and Students in Civil, Commercial, Business, Property, Workplace, and Employment Cases' by Jonathan Dingle with John Sephton
'The Mini-Pupillage Workbook' by David Boyle
'A Practical Guide to Crofting Law' by Brian Inkster
'A Practical Guide to Spousal Maintenance' by Liz Cowell
'A Practical Guide to the Law of Domain Names and Cybersquatting' by Andrew Clemson
'A Practical Guide to the Law of Gender Pay Gap Reporting' by Harini Iyengar
'A Practical Guide to the Rights of Grandparents in Children Proceedings' by Stuart Barlow
'NHS Whistleblowing and the Law' by Joseph England
'Employment Law and the Gig Economy' by Nigel Mackay & Annie Powell
'A Practical Guide to Noise Induced Hearing Loss (NIHL) Claims' by Andrew Mckie, Ian Skeate, Gareth McAloon
'An Introduction to Beauty Negligence Claims – A Practical Guide for the Personal Injury Practitioner' by Greg Almond
'Intercompany Agreements for Transfer Pricing Compliance' by Paul Sutton
'Zen and the Art of Mediation' by Martin Plowman
'A Practical Guide to the SRA Principles, Individual and Law Firm Codes of Conduct 2019 – What Every Law Firm Needs to Know' by Paul Bennett
'A Practical Guide to Adoption for Family Lawyers' by Graham Pegg
'A Practical Guide to Industrial Disease Claims' by Andrew Mckie & Ian Skeate
'A Practical Guide to Redundancy' by Philip Hyland
'A Practical Guide to Vicarious Liability' by Mariel Irvine
'A Practical Guide to Applications for Landlord's Consent and Variation of Leases' by Mark Shelton
'A Practical Guide to Relief from Sanctions Post-Mitchell and Denton' by Peter Causton
'A Practical Guide to Equity Release for Advisors' by Paul Sams
'A Practical Guide to Financial Services Claims' by Chris Hegarty

'The Law of Houses in Multiple Occupation: A Practical Guide to HMO Proceedings' by Julian Hunt

'Occupiers, Highways and Defective Premises Claims: A Practical Guide Post-Jackson – 2nd Edition' by Andrew Mckie

'A Practical Guide to Financial Ombudsman Service Claims' by Adam Temple & Robert Scrivenor

'A Practical Guide to Advising Schools on Employment Law' by Jonathan Holden

'A Practical Guide to Running Housing Disrepair and Cavity Wall Claims: 2nd Edition' by Andrew Mckie & Ian Skeate

'A Practical Guide to Holiday Sickness Claims – 2nd Edition' by Andrew Mckie & Ian Skeate

'Arguments and Tactics for Personal Injury and Clinical Negligence Claims' by Dorian Williams

'A Practical Guide to Drone Law' by Rufus Ballaster, Andrew Firman, Eleanor Clot

'A Practical Guide to Compliance for Personal Injury Firms Working With Claims Management Companies' by Paul Bennett

'RTA Allegations of Fraud in a Post-Jackson Era: The Handbook – 2nd Edition' by Andrew Mckie

'RTA Personal Injury Claims: A Practical Guide Post-Jackson' by Andrew Mckie

'On Experts: CPR35 for Lawyers and Experts' by David Boyle

'An Introduction to Personal Injury Law' by David Boyle

'A Practical Guide to Subtle Brain Injury Claims' by Pankaj Madan

These books and more are available to order online direct from the publisher at www.lawbriefpublishing.com, where you can also read free sample chapters. For any queries, contact us on 0844 587 2383 or mail@lawbriefpublishing.com.

Our books are also usually in stock at www.amazon.co.uk with free next day delivery for Prime members, and at good legal bookshops such as Wildy & Sons.

We are regularly launching new books in our series of practical day-to-day practitioners' guides. Visit our website and join our free newsletter to be kept informed and to receive special offers, free chapters, etc.

You can also follow us on Twitter at www.twitter.com/lawbriefpub.

www.ingramcontent.com/pod-product-compliance
Lightning Source LLC
LaVergne TN
LVHW022107200926
848481LV00003B/1086
9781914608360